MECHWARRI4R
VENGEANCE

Sybex OFFICIAL
Strategies & Secrets™

Doug Radcliffe
and David Ellis

SYBEX®

San Francisco • Paris • Düsseldorf • Soest • London

W9-AVN-285

Associate Publisher: DAN BRODNITZ
Contracts and Licensing Manager: KRISTINE O'CALLAGHAN
Acquisitions and Developmental Editor: STEVE ANDERSON
Managing Editor Game Books: ROGER BURCHILL
Editor: BRETT TODD
Production Editor: MARISA ONG
Proofreader: ANDREA FOX
Book Design: MUELLER DESIGN INTERACTIVE
Book Production: WILLIAM SALIT DESIGN
Production Assistant: LISA LUSK
Cover Design: VICTOR ARRE
Poster Design: WILLIAM SALIT DESIGN

SYBEX and the SYBEX logo are either registered trademarks or trademarks of SYBEX, Inc. in the United States and/or other countries.

Strategies & Secrets is a trademark of SYBEX, Inc.

MechWarrior, BattleTech, BattleMech, and 'Mech are either registered trademarks or trademarks of FASA Corporation and/or Microsoft Corporation in the United States and/or other countries.

Microsoft, Windows, and Microsoft MechWarrior: Vengeance are either registered trademarks or trademarks of Microsoft Corporation in the United States and/or other countries.

Microsoft and Windows are either registered trademarks or trademarks of Microsoft Corporation in the United States and/or other countries. © 1998–2001 Microsoft Corporation. All rights reserved.

TRADEMARKS: Sybex has attempted throughout this book to distinguish proprietary trademarks from descriptive terms by following the capitalization style used by the manufacturer.

The author and publisher have made their best efforts to prepare this book. Game content is subject to change after its release. The author and the publisher make no representation or warranties of any kind with regard to the completeness or accuracy of the contents herein and accept no liability of any kind including but not limited to performance, merchantability, fitness for any particular purpose, or any losses or damages of any kind caused or alleged to be caused directly or indirectly from this book.

Copyright©2000 SYBEX, Inc., 1151 Marina Village Parkway, Alameda, CA 94501. World rights reserved. No part of this publication may be stored in a retrieval system, transmitted, or reproduced in any way, including but not limited to photocopy, photograph, magnetic or other record, without the prior agreement and written permission of the publisher.

Library of Congress Card Number: 00-109110

ISBN: 0-7821-2867-X

Manufactured in the United States of America

10 9 8 7 6 5 4 3 2 1

In dedication to crmbt... "boos rockets."
—D.R.

To Meghan—as always, thanks for supporting me in everything I do.
—D.E.

acknowledgments

A big thanks to the Sybex team, whose unwavering support and patience continues to impress. Thanks to Steve Anderson, Dan Brodnitz, and Willem Knibbe—all of you provided essential help during the course of the project and I offer many thanks. Thanks also to copy editor Brett Todd for keeping me on my toes and Marisa Ong for her superior production skills.

Congratulations to the *MechWarrior 4: Vengeance* team at Microsoft® for putting together a worthy sequel! For their generous assistance and contributions to this guide, special thanks must go out to T.J. Wagner, David Abzug, Christopher Blohm, James Mayo, Derek Carroll, Tim Znamenacek, Todd Lubsen, Jon Kimmich, Peter Parsons, Justin Kirby, Steve Fowler, Michael Turner, Shaleen Pruitt, and Keith Cirillo. At Microsoft Games, thanks are also due Melethia Campbell and Kellini Walter.

Finally, a huge thanks to David Ellis for his impressive additions to the book—thanks for coming through in the clutch!

—D.R.

Not to be repetitive, but thanks to everyone at Sybex—Steve Anderson, Dan Brodnitz, and Marisa Ong—for bringing me in on this project and supporting my efforts along the way. Also, a huge thanks to Doug Radcliffe for letting me add my small contribution to his book. It's been a pleasure!

—D.E.

A Letter from the Publisher

Dear Reader,

At Sybex, our goal is to bring you the best game strategy guides money can buy. We hire the best authors in the business, and we bring our love of games to the look and feel of the books. We hope you see all of that reflected in the strategy guide you're holding in your hands right now.

The important question is: How well do YOU think we're doing?

Are we providing you with the kind of in-depth, hardcore gaming content you crave? Is the material presented in a way you find both useful and attractive? Are there other approaches and/or types of information you'd like to see but just aren't getting? Or, are our books so perfect that you're considering nominating them for a Pulitzer this year?

Your comments and suggestions are always valuable. We want to encourage even more feedback from our readers and make it even easier for you to get in touch with us. To that end, we've created an e-mailbox for your feedback. We invite you to send your comments, criticism, praise, and suggestions to gamesfeedback@sybex.com and let us know what you think.

We can't guarantee we'll respond to every message; but we can promise we'll read them all, take them to heart, and then print them out and use the hard copy to make festive hats for everyone in the building.

Most of all, we'll use your feedback to continuously improve the quality of our books. So please, let us hear from you!

Dan Brodnitz
Associate Publisher

Contents

contents

contents

contents

contents

contents

introduction

Welcome to Microsoft's MechWarrior® 4: Vengeance! Developed by the creators of the BattleTech® Universe and the original MechWarrior game, MechWarrior 4: Vengeance portrays the players' epic struggles as they command heavily armed war machines known as BattleMechs® across the remote battlefields of hostile worlds.

Surviving this dangerous terrain requires the expertise you'll only find in this official Strategies & Secrets guide, written with the full support of the Microsoft design teams. Inside this official guide, you'll discover an in-depth analysis for piloting, controlling your BattleMech's onboard systems, and sending your 'Mech® into battle. Comprehensive statistics and tactics are included for all 21 BattleMechs (including the seven new 'Mechs) and all weapon types. A complete walkthrough for the single-player campaign has been included, along with strategies for competing online in all of MechWarrior 4: Vengeance's multiplayer game modes.

Story Timeline

To provide a brief background to the story told in *MechWarrior 4: Vengeance*, here's a timeline of events:

A.D. 3028: Prince Hanse Davion marries Archon Designate Melissa Steiner, cementing an alliance between two of the most powerful realms in the Inner Sphere of known space: the Federated Suns and the Lyran Commonwealth. Their eldest son, Victor, stands to inherit a unified state consisting of hundreds of star systems. The Fourth Succession War begins, damaging the Draconis Combine and crippling the Capellan Confederation.

A.D. 3050: A new threat forces the states of the Inner Sphere to set aside their differences. The Clans, descendants of the ancient armies of the Star League, sweep in with superior technology and training, leaving a trail of crushed and broken BattleMechs behind them. The Draconis Combine takes the brunt of the attack.

A.D. 3052: Comstar, the independent body controlling interstellar communications, forces the Clans to halt their advance. That same year, Hanse Davion dies of a heart attack in his office. Doctors attribute this to stress, though some still suspect foul play. Victor takes up the reins of the Federated Suns, vowing to prepare his realm for the day when Comstar's treaty expires.

A.D. 3055: After offering to abdicate and surrender the Lyran Commonwealth to her son, Victor, Melissa Steiner is assassinated. The conspirator behind the assassination is never found. The Commonwealth goes into mourning over the loss of its much-beloved Archon.

A.D. 3056: The Federated Commonwealth is officially formed. Victor Steiner-Davion takes control as Archon-Prince, fulfilling his destiny of ruling the most powerful realm in the Inner Sphere. While tensions remain high, conflict is limited to minor border skirmishes.

A.D. 3057: Victor's sister, Katherine, takes the Lyran half of the realm. Assuming the name Katrina Steiner, after their grandmother, she declares herself Archon of the new Lyran Alliance. The same year, Clan Wolf fights its epic Trial of Refusal with Clan Jade Falcon. Both clans are decimated in the end, and Katrina grants sanctuary to the fleeing remnants of Clan Wolf.

A.D. 3058: Victor engineers the formation of a new Star League. Its first order of business: the elimination of Clan Smoke Jaguar. Two massive forces, one led by Morgan Hasek-Davion and the other by Victor Davion, strike at the invading clan. When the dust settles, Clan Smoke Jaguar is no more.

The present: While Victor has been away at war, Katrina has moved to take control of the remainder of his realm. Loyalist units are being subverted or destroyed, including the noble Dresari family on Kentares IV.

Your mission begins on the cold, harsh Kentares IV moon. Supplies and BattleMechs are limited. You must operate and complete mission objectives under these constraints as the resistance gains strength. But as supplies become more plentiful, the missions and objectives become harder. Prepare for a long, tough war in *MechWarrior 4: Vengeance*!

How to Use This Book

Sybex's official *MechWarrior 4: Vengeance: Strategies & Secrets* is divided into four distinct sections to best serve your needs. Consider this guide the definitive handbook for all aspiring 'Mech pilots. Should you need to brush up on your combat skills, turn to Part 1: Combat Training. Need some detailed statistics and strategies on all the hardware you'll encounter? Flip to Part 2: 'Mechs, Vehicles, and Weapons. If you're looking for tips on completing the single-player operations, proceed to Part 3: Campaign Walkthrough to find all the information you need.

Part 1: Combat Training

In Chapter 1: Taking Control, you'll learn the essential techniques for taking charge of your BattleMech. Topics include mastering the controls, managing heat, using sensors, and commanding lancemates in battle. The chapter also includes vital lancemate statistics and how to determine their worth in battle situations.

Chapter 2: Combat Tactics 101 focuses solely on how to best guide your BattleMech in combat situations. Here you will learn offensive and defensive skills, situation-specific tactics, special combat maneuvers (including ramming, ambushing, and death from above), salvaging techniques, how to take advantage of the environmental effects on combat, and about grouping and targeting weapons.

Part 2: 'Mechs, Vehicles, and Weapons

Chapter 3: BattleMechs and Non-'Mech Vehicles gives the lowdown on all 21 'Mechs available in *MechWarrior 4: Vengeance*. Each entry includes vital statistics, including armor layout and default weaponry, and proven strategies for using each on the battlefield. A brief section at the end of the chapter details statistics for the non-'Mech vehicles encountered in the game.

In Chapter 4: Weapons and Components, you'll find *MechWarrior 4: Vengeance*'s complete arsenal of laser, ballistic, and missile-based weaponry. The chapter describes the function, strengths, and weaknesses of all the weapons and other 'Mech components, as well as statistics for all items and strategies for their use.

Part 3: Campaign Walkthrough

The seven chapters that make up Part 3: Campaign Walkthrough present guides for all the single-player operations and missions. Each walkthrough includes the mission briefing, full list of objectives, recommended MechLab configuration, and a proven solution with specific battle tactics. The walkthroughs here present a complete, but by all means not the only, solution to each challenge that you'll face during the campaign.

Chapter 5 includes walkthroughs for the four lunar-based missions that comprise Operation 1: "Optimism." The four arctic-based missions that make up Operation 2: "Early Success" are detailed in Chapter 6. Chapter 7 features the three alpine-based mission walkthroughs included within Operation 3: "First Command."

Walkthroughs for the six desert-based missions forming Operation 4: "Building Forces" take up the majority of Chapter 8. In Chapter 9, you'll find walkthroughs for the three swamp-based missions included in Operation 5: "The Greater Good." Chapter 10 features the urban-based mission walkthroughs making up Operation 6, "The Darkest Hour."

Chapter 11 features the mission walkthrough for the final mission, "End Game," the sole assignment in the palace-based Operation 7: "Final Victory."

Part 4: Multiplayer Strategies

Strategies for competing in head-to-head online play, either in a free-for-all or in a team battle, can be found in Part 4: Multiplayer Strategies. The tactics detailed within include *MechWarrior 4: Vengeance*'s popular free-for-all modes Attrition, Destruction, King of the Hill, and Steal the Beacon, as well as general techniques used to battle a crafty human opponent.

TIP

Be sure to visit the Sybex Games Web site at www.sybexgames.com for free online updates and additional strategies for *MechWarrior 4: Vengeance*.

Chapter 13 shifts the focus to team-based MechWarrior combat. Specific strategies for Team Attrition, Capture the Flag, Team Destruction, Escort, and Team King of the Hill are brought into focus here.

part 1

combat training

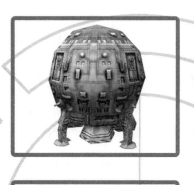

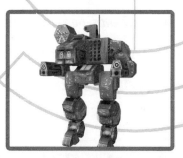

Proper basic training is the key to success in MechWarrior 4: Vengeance. Even the most detailed mission walkthrough can't take you very far if you don't have a good working knowledge of rudimentary control and combat techniques. Taking control of a 'Mech without proper training and attempting to follow a walkthrough is like jumping into a car and trying to read a road map before learning how to drive!

Part 1 of this guide is dedicated to teaching you how to handle your 'Mech like an expert. Here you'll learn basic control techniques, weapon strategies, and combat strategies that will prepare you for the difficult missions that lie ahead. You'll also learn some interesting and innovative battle maneuvers that are guaranteed to surprise and befuddle your enemies in both the campaign game and in multiplayer confrontations.

When you've finished this section, you'll have the basic knowledge you need to begin your career as a MechWarrior.

making control

You are about to take control of a BattleMech, one of the most powerful war machines ever created. This towering metal beast weighs more than a present-day tank and moves at almost twice the speed. Sitting in the cockpit of a 'Mech is not particularly difficult in and of itself, but controlling it effectively in battle requires skill and practice.

In this chapter, we'll look at some of the basic things you'll deal with as a pilot, and help you get a handle on some of the skills you'll need to make the transition from raw recruit to full-fledged MechWarrior. When it comes to learning 'Mech functions and controls, nothing beats hands-on experience. Before you dive headfirst into the campaign or a multiplayer skirmish, take some time to run through the Instant Action tutorial mission, where you'll receive step-by-step instruction on all aspects of basic 'Mech operations.

Mastering the Controls

As you've no doubt noticed by looking at your manual, *MechWarrior 4: Vengeance* has a *lot* of controls. In order to play effectively, you'll need to access most of your 'Mech's vital functions without looking down at the keyboard. A momentary distraction from the screen can mean the difference between life and death in the middle of a battle.

Before embarking on the campaign or plunging into an online battle, take your 'Mech for an Instant Action test run and familiarize yourself with the control layout. That way, once you're in the heat of combat, you'll be ready for any situation that arises.

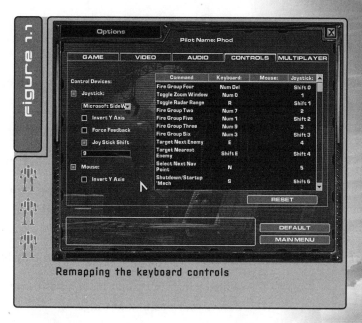

figure 1.1

Remapping the keyboard controls

Can't seem to get the hang of things? Don't like the way the controls are laid out? You're in luck. The game allows you to remap the keys and buttons to suit your needs and preferences (see Figure 1.1). If you decide to do this, we recommend that you map all of your most commonly used controls in such a way so as to be accessible with one hand (whichever one you're not using for the joystick or mouse). The exact configuration is up to you, but set things up so that looking at the keyboard during a battle situation is kept to an absolute minimum.

By the way, although you can play *MechWarrior 4* with the keyboard and mouse, we *highly* recommend that you use a joystick (preferably one with a throttle) for the best possible control over your 'Mech. With a joystick, most of the common controls are mapped to the buttons and are right at your fingertips at all times.

Basic 'Mech Operation

Between the manual and the training missions included in the game, you already have a basic idea of how your BattleMech's systems work. Here we'll look at a few of those systems in more detail and teach you a few tricks that will make your life as a MechWarrior a little easier.

Using Your Sensors

Every 'Mech is equipped with a basic sensor package. This allows you to detect other units and lock your missiles onto targets. Some essential facts you should know about basic sensors include:

- All mobile units with weapons have basic sensors.

- All basic sensors are identical in range and function.

- Basic sensors can be temporarily disrupted by strong electromagnetic fields (power lines and generators, for example) and by nearby explosions.

- Shutdown 'Mechs cannot be detected by basic sensors.

- When active (in default mode), basic sensors help other units detect *your* position at range.

You have the option of switching your sensors off. This tactic is known as "going passive." When you go passive, your radar goes dead, your targeting system ceases to function, and you can't lock missiles on target. The only advantage to running in passive mode is that it halves the distance at which your enemies can detect your presence. This is a useful tactic when you're trying to sneak up on a foe. At the same time, however, this greatly increases the risk that someone could sneak up on *you*. Unless you're going for a stealthy approach, you should leave your sensors active at all times.

Some 'Mechs can be equipped with advanced sensor equipment that improves the performance of their own sensors or inhibits those of the enemy. A few select 'Mechs actually have this high-tech gear included in their default loadout (see Chapter 3: BattleMechs and Non-'Mech Vehicles for more). Advanced sensor hardware comes in two varieties:

- **Beagle Active Probe:** The twin functions of this handy item are to increase your active sensor range and reduce the amount of time it takes to lock missiles on an enemy target by 30%. It is also impervious to the electromagnetic interference that affects basic sensors. The downside to this device is that, when in use, its emissions allow enemies to lock *their* missiles on *you* 30% faster as well.

Guardian ECM: This device doesn't enhance your sensors. Instead, it inhibits your enemies' ability to detect you at range, effectively giving your 'Mech a stealth mode. Guardian ECM also limits the usefulness of enemy NARC Beacons. It has two notable drawbacks, however. First, like the Beagle Active Probe, it improves enemy missile lock time by 30%. Second, it ceases to function when you're using your Jump Jets and any time your heat level rises above 50%.

> Both the Beagle and the Guardian ECM systems can be extremely useful, but they turn you into a missile magnet—especially if you have both systems mounted (since the missile lock effects are cumulative). If you know you'll be up against 'Mechs that don't have missiles, these systems are great enhancements. Otherwise, think twice before investing the weight and space they take up.

The availability of these systems is restricted by 'Mech type, so the decision of whether or not to use them is often not in your hands. The breakdown is as follows:

Raven and Loki 'Mechs can use both systems.

Hellspawn, Thanatos, Atlas, Vulture, and Thor designs can mount only the Guardian ECM system.

Uziel, Argus, Catapult, Mauler, Cougar, Shadow Cat, Nova Cat, Mad Cat, and Mad Cat MK. II can use only the Beagle Active Probe.

Osiris, Chimera, Bushwacker, Awesome, and Daishi can't be equipped with either system.

Table 1.1 shows maximum sensor ranges under a variety of game conditions.

Table 1.1: sensor ranges (in meters)

Condition	Target Is Shut Down	Target Has Sensors Off	Target Has Basic Sensors	Target Has ECM
Sensing 'Mech Is Shut Down	0	0	0	0
Sensing 'Mech Has Sensors Off	0	0	250	100
Sensing 'Mech Has Basic Sensors	0	500	1000	500
Sensing 'Mech Has Active Probe	100	600	1200	800

Movement Nuances

One of the most difficult things to master in *MechWarrior 4* is moving your 'Mech. Most of the mistakes that lead to poor combat performance and (ultimately) your destruction come down to not maneuvering effectively. There are two basic situations to consider here: moving from encounter to encounter and combat movement. Here are some techniques to keep in mind.

When moving between encounters:

Keep your torso pointed in the direction you're moving. It is extremely disorienting to move one way while facing another. It's also not the best way to encounter the enemy. Use the "look" controls to scan the terrain rather than twisting your 'Mech's torso to do so.

Keep an eye on your allies. It's easy to lose track of your comrades if you're moving full-tilt toward a waypoint. Use your radar and look controls to keep an eye on your companions. That way, when you reach your objective, you won't find that you're facing the enemy alone because you've left your lancemates in the dust. Better still, fall back so you're slightly behind them. That way, they get hit first if there's something nasty around the next hill.

When maneuvering in combat:

Torso twisting is key. While you need to face an enemy in order to fight, your options are terribly limited if you can only move toward and away from your target. Use your torso twist to face the enemy while circling him (preferably out of his weapon arc). This orientation also allows you to protect one of your 'Mech's legs at all times by keeping it away from the enemy (see Figure 1.2).

Keep your hand on the throttle. Speed is often the key to survival in combat, especially for smaller 'Mechs—but you can't expect to fight effectively with the throttle wide open all the time. The key to effective combat positioning is to maintain constant control over your speed and direction, always making adjustments to match your enemy's speed and directional changes.

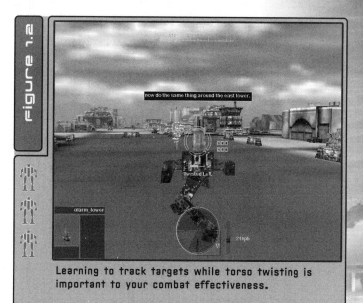

Backing away isn't a bad thing. If you're fighting a 'Mech with lots of short-range weapons, your enemy will try to stay close to you. Recognizing this tactic and responding by backing away is vital to surviving these encounters.

Once again, we can't stress enough the importance of practice when it comes to getting the feel of your 'Mech. This is especially true when trying to master movement control. Spend a lot of time in the tutorial mission, trying out your moves and honing them.

Figure 1.2

now do the same thing around the east tower.

Twisted Left

alarm_tower

21kph

Learning to track targets while torso twisting is important to your combat effectiveness.

Heat Management

One of the most critical skills to master as a MechWarrior is heat management. Every 'Mech in the game has a heat scale. Let the gauge rise too high, and you'll encounter serious equipment problems. Although the loadout and design of your 'Mech ultimately determine its heat efficiency, your role in heat management is important in almost every battle situation. (If you absolutely don't want to deal with overheating, you can turn it off in the game options. You can then fire your weapons with impunity and be none the worse for it.)

Cause and Effect

The two most common things that cause your 'Mech to heat up are weapons and movement. Weapons fire, however, is the primary culprit. Every weapon is rated for heat (see the table in Chapter 4: Weapons and Components). Each warms up at varying degrees depending on both this rating and your rate of fire.

Movement is the lesser of two evils when it comes to heat and, under most circumstances, doesn't present too much of a problem. When moving at up to half of its top speed, a 'Mech builds up one point of heat per second. It builds up two points per second at any speed higher than that. The worst form of movement as far as heat is concerned is jumping. While a 'Mech's Jump Jets are engaged, heat builds up at a rate of four points per second.

As a 'Mech warms up, it loses combat effectiveness (see Figure 1.3). Heat problems manifest themselves in a variety of ways:

NOTE

The game defines a weapon's heat rating as a numeric value, but your 'Mech measures heat in degrees. For the sake of easy reference, each point of a weapon's heat rating is roughly equal to 167 degrees.

- **Loss of torso twist speed:** When heat rises above the 30% mark, a 'Mech's torso twist speed decreases.

- **Loss of movement speed:** As the heat scale passes the 50% mark, a 'Mech's maximum speed begins to degrade. The higher the heat, the slower the BattleMech.

- **HUD deterioration:** When heat is above 50%, the HUD becomes more difficult to read.

- **Total shutdown:** Any time heat is above the 50% mark, there is a possibility that your 'Mech will shut down entirely. The

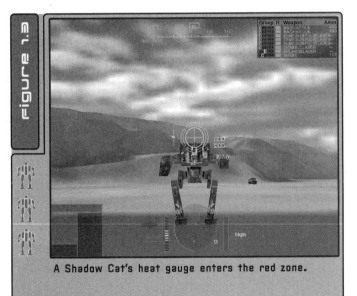

Figure 1.3

A Shadow Cat's heat gauge enters the red zone.

higher the heat, the more likely the shutdown. If your temperature remains at the 100% mark for more than a second, systems go down immediately. Once this occurs, the 'Mech cannot be restarted until the heat level has been below 80% for five seconds.

NOTE

Heat-related failure occurs when a 'Mech's temperature exceeds the system failure's minimum heat threshold for more than two seconds. Brief spikes in heat have no effect.

Heat Dissipation Strategies

'Mechs have two built-in methods for dealing with heat buildup: heat sinks and coolant flush. Every 'Mech is equipped with a number of heat sinks that are built into its engine. Each dissipates two points of heat per second. Thus, a 'Mech with 10 heat sinks dissipates 20 points of heat per second.

The other method is flushing coolant through the 'Mech's systems. This cools one point of heat per gallon of coolant used. Coolant flushing should be used sparingly, however, because a 'Mech's supply of this vital fluid is extremely limited. The exact amount of coolant available varies depending on the 'Mech.

The most effective method of heat management is to simply monitor your heat levels. If you see your temperature approaching the danger zone, immediately take one or more of the following steps:

- **Slow down.** As noted above, you build up less heat at lower speeds.

- **Don't jump.** Frequent use of your Jump Jets greatly compounds an overheat situation.

- **Stop shooting.** Admittedly, this isn't always possible. But if a problem arises in the midst of a firefight, try to escape the battle until your heat is under control.

- **Fire weapons individually.** While linking weapons is a quick way to inflict lots of damage, the more weapons you fire simultaneously, the faster your heat builds up.

- **Stick to "cool" weapons:** When your temperature is high, fire only the weaponry that produces the least heat. As a rule of thumb, the order of weapons from coolest to hottest is ballistic weapons, missiles, and beam weapons.

> **TIP**
>
> If you find yourself constantly dealing with overheating problems, chances are your 'Mech is poorly designed. By visiting the MechLab and adding a few additional heat sinks (or changing your weapons loadout to include cooler weapons), you can save yourself a lot of headaches.

The final thing to keep in mind is that the battlefield environment can affect your 'Mech's ability to dissipate heat. Heat sink efficiency is affected by the following factors:

- **Ambient temperature:** Hot environments (such as lava flows and deserts) decrease heat sink efficiency, while cold environments (such as arctic zones and moons) increase your ability to dissipate heat.

- **Rain:** Heat sinks operate more effectively in the rain.

- **Environmental objects and localized events:** Certain objects are hot by nature, but don't cast their heat over a wide area. While standing near such an object—an ore smelter, for instance—your heat sinks are less efficient. Other localized conditions (like fires and explosions) also affect your 'Mech's heat dissipation capabilities when you're in close proximity to them.

If a large body of water is nearby, you have a quick and easy (albeit temporary) solution to any heat problem. Entering a large body of water increases heat sink efficiency—the deeper the water, the faster the heat dissipates (see Figure 1.4.).

Keep your cool by taking your 'Mech for a swim.

Controlling Your Lancemates

Throughout the campaign, you will encounter MechWarriors who join in your quest to free Kentares IV. These comrades, known as lancemates, show up in a variety of circumstances and are often available to assist you in missions (see Figure 1.5).

Starting with the first mission of Operation 2: "Early Success," you can usually select at least one lancemate to accompany you into battle. Lancemates are your wingmen and are there

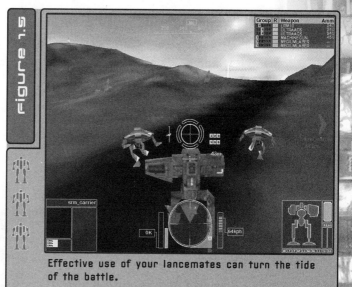

Effective use of your lancemates can turn the tide of the battle.

to support you—but they can only do so effectively if you know how to use them properly.

NOTE

Don't be confused by the fact that you are often accompanied into battle by allies you *can't* control. Before Operation 2, your lancemates work autonomously and will not respond to orders.

Basic Commands and Behavior

Lancemates have sets of statistics that govern behavior in combat. Even if you don't issue specific orders, they'll follow your lead and stick with you to the best of their abilities. When an armed enemy comes into range, your lancemates automatically engage the target and keep fighting until they're told otherwise. They'll attack unarmed foes, too, provided that they're part of the mission objective.

Just letting your lancemates tag along for the ride isn't a very effective way to use them. They operate best when given specific orders. *MechWarrior 4* includes nine commands you can issue to your lancemates in battle:

- **Attack My Target:** This is, by far, the most useful command. Use it to assign specific targets for your lancemates to concentrate on. Unless you're attacking something particularly big or powerful, you should always assign your lancemates different targets than the one you intend to take out yourself.

- **Defend My Target:** This command orders your lancemates to defend a selected friendly unit or building. Use this command *only* if the unit or building's survival is critical to the success of the mission. Otherwise, your lancemates are better utilized in a more aggressive role.

- **Form Up On Me:** This command can save your lancemates' lives. When you give an attack or defend order, your allies are quite single-minded about following it; they'll continue fighting to the best of their abilities

TIP

The best thing your lancemates provide is additional targets for your enemies to shoot at. This might seem callous, but it's true. Send your allies off to attack different targets than the one you're concentrating on—that way, you'll have fewer enemies aiming at you.

even when critically damaged. This order tells them to follow you, thus rescuing them from dangerous (if not suicidal) situations.

Hold Fire: This command is only useful when you know your lancemate is low on ammunition; issuing this order is foolhardy in most situations. Remember that it leaves your lancemates unable to defend themselves.

Go To My Nav Point: This command is quite handy. If you want to protect yourself, send your lancemates ahead to scout the area and engage the enemy before you wade in with your own 'Mech. Just remember that lancemates cannot stray more than 350 meters from your position.

NOTE

Your lancemates can't be killed until Operation 4. Until that time, they automatically eject safely if their 'Mechs are destroyed. Even in Operation 4 and beyond, several lancemates are key to the campaign and always survive.

Report Your Status: As mentioned earlier, your lancemates fight on no matter what their condition. Unfortunately, they don't usually give you much warning when their 'Mechs are getting chewed up. Therefore, you should periodically check on their condition.

Shutdown: The only thing worse than ordering a lancemate to Hold Fire is ordering him to Shutdown—it leaves your ally not only unable to fire but unable to avoid being hit! Unless you have an airtight strategy in mind, avoid this command at all costs.

Attack Nearest Enemy: This obvious command is one that an operational lancemate carries out automatically if he hasn't received orders to the contrary.

One rather effective, if risky, strategy involves using the Shutdown and Attack Nearest Enemy commands to set up an ambush for an approaching enemy unit. Order a lancemate to shut his 'Mech down between you and an oncoming foe. Distract this opponent with an attack of your own, then order the shutdown lancemate to "Attack Nearest Enemy" as soon as the enemy is in range. The danger here is that the enemy might launch an attack on the shutdown 'Mech, which is completely defenseless until you order it to attack. Also, this feint only works against enemies with basic sensors.

Repair At Nearest Spot: The advantages of this command are obvious. Whenever a Mobile Field Base (MFB) or Repair Bay is available, you can order damaged lancemates to find the nearest one and proceed there to fix their damage. However, before you give this order, you must weigh the advantage of a fully repaired lancemate against the disadvantage of not having your ally around for part of the mission.

When accompanied by multiple lancemates, you should issue commands individually rather than to everyone simultaneously. Unless you need all your allies to rally at your position or attack a single tough target, the fine control you achieve by transmitting orders individually provides more tactical leeway and forces your enemy to likewise split up his or her forces in response.

> **TIP**
>
> A tenth command, Capture Enemy's Flag, is available in multiplayer Capture the Flag games. Using this command is a great way to set up a feint to occupy your opponent while you make a grab for the flag yourself.

Lancemate Skills

An important part of learning how to properly control your lancemates is knowing exactly what each is capable of. Every lancemate has his or her own personality, which determines actions and reactions during combat. But more importantly (and less visibly) each also has a set of statistics that determines how well he or she performs in battle. These statistics, known as "skills," are divided into two categories: basic and special.

The basic skills are as follows:

Piloting: This determines the percentage chance for the lancemate's 'Mech to fall. This skill is checked when the 'Mech takes heavy damage, uses the death from above tactic (as described in Chapter 2: Combat Tactics 101), is hit by numerous shots from the same direction, steps off the edge of a high object, or messes up a jump landing.

Gunnery: This skill helps judge a lancemate's base chance to hit. Range and speed figure into the final calculation, but the higher the Gunnery rating, the better the lancemate's chance to hit a target under any circumstances.

Sensors: This number determines how frequently the lancemate checks his or her sensors. The best possible rating is two.

Elite Level/Tactical Knowledge: The number and complexity of tactical maneuvers the lancemate can perform in battle are gauged here. The higher this stat, the more adept the lancemate is at combat tactics.

Maximum/Minimum Heat Level: Your lancemate's reaction to his or her 'Mech's temperature is calculated with this score. Whenever the heat level reaches the specified maximum, the lancemate stops firing and won't fire again until the heat drops to the specified minimum.

> **TIP**
> Your lancemates' Piloting, Gunnery, Sensors, and Elite Level/Tactical Knowledge skills improve every time you include them in a mission. By selecting the same lancemates for multiple missions, you can significantly increase their usefulness.

Special skills are modifiers applied to your lancemates' Gunnery skill under special combat circumstances. They include:

Blind Fighting: The ability to attack targets at night or beyond the lancemate's maximum visibility range.

Long-Range Gunnery: The ability of a lancemate to attack targets at ranges of 600 meters or greater.

Short-Range Gunnery: The ability to attack targets at ranges of 300 meters or less.

Special skills do not increase as a result of experience.

You can view your lancemates' current statistics prior to a mission by selecting them in the Lancemate Selection screen. Their stats are also viewable both during (by selecting the lancemate as a target) and after battle, though the post-mission report omits the lancemates' special skill ratings.

While there is no way for you to know the exact numeric special skill ratings for your lancemates, you can estimate their special skill bonus using the breakdown shown in Table 1.2. Positive values add to the lancemate's ability in a given situation, while negative values detract from it.

Table 1.2: Special Skill Numeric Breakdown

Skill Rating	Special Skill Bonus
Poor	-30 or lower
Below Average	-29 to -11
Average	-10 to 10
Good	11 to 25
Superior	26 to 40
Outstanding	41 or higher

combat Tactics 101

Now that you've learned the basics of 'Mech control, it's time to put those skills to the test in the heat of combat. The first time you come face to face with an enemy 'Mech can be an overwhelming experience. Unless you're really lucky, chances are you'll end up dead—or, at the very least, you'll limp away from the encounter with your 'Mech badly damaged.

In this chapter, we'll impart some basic tips on how to survive in the field. The hints and strategies you learn here will give you a strong foundation of knowledge that you can put to practical use in any game situation.

Environmental Issues

Something you need to consider, even before you bring your weapons to bear, is the battlefield itself. The area where you'll be doing battle can significantly affect the performance of your 'Mech. Terrain will often be a deciding factor in what tactics you'll be able to use effectively.

Six basic environmental types and one very unique one are present in *MechWarrior 4*:

- **Moon/Lunar:** This stark environment is nearly as bleak as Earth's lone satellite. Moons mostly feature packed dirt surfaces, hills, and mountains. When fighting in such terrain, you'll have little or no problem with heat buildup in your 'Mech. The earliest missions in the campaign game take place in a lunar environment.

- **Tundra:** Tundra landscapes feature some trees and sparse vegetation, and are thus less barren than the lunar variety, but the conditions are otherwise very similar. Heat is more of a factor here than on a moon, but is still less pressing than in other environments.

- **Desert:** Deserts aren't the bleak wastelands you might expect. They're actually much like the outskirts of large, southwestern cities, with scattered buildings and man-made facilities in the vicinity. Although overheating is more of a problem than in other environments, deserts often have large bodies of water, which you can use to dissipate excess heat.

- **Marshlands/Swamps:** The most diverse environments in the game, marshlands include forests, swamps, beaches, and rolling grassland. Again, lots of water is available for heat management purposes.

- **Light Forest:** Almost as varied as marshlands, light forests include wooded areas, hills, mountains, and even occasional patches of snow.

- **Urban:** Urban settings are the downtown areas of huge cities. As such, they're the most confined environment to be encountered in the game. Terrain types are generally concrete and rough.

- **Palace:** The final mission takes place in and around a huge, ornate palace. Expect a combination of wide-open and claustrophobic combat here on just about any terrain type imaginable.

Within these environmental areas, you'll find lots of different terrain types. Each of these can affect unit movement capabilities and the amount of cover available. Terrain types are classified as follows:

- **Dirt/Grass:** Any firm, natural surface.

- **Concrete:** Smooth, man-made surfaces. This includes paved roads, tarmac, and so on.

- **Rough:** Hard, broken terrain with chunks too small to block 'Mech movement. Concrete blocks, boulders, and such will be scattered about.

- **Snow:** A region with snow deep enough to cover a 'Mech's ankles. Shallower snow is treated in the game as grass.

- **Thick Underbrush:** High vegetation, thick bushes, and so on.

◄● **Shallow Water:** Features water up to a 'Mech's ankles in depth.

◄● **Mid-Water:** Water with a depth ranging from above a 'Mech's ankles to just over its head.

◄● **Oceanic Depths:** Really deep water.

◄● **Flat Swamp:** Thick, muddy water with no large obstacles.

◄● **Thick Swamp:** Same as the above but with obstacles such as trees, bushes, rocks, logs, and so on.

Table 2.1 shows the effects of each terrain type on 'Mechs and other vehicles.

Table 2.1: Terrain Effects on 'Mechs and Vehicles

Terrain	'Mech Speed	Wheeled Speed	Tracked Speed	Additional 'Mech Effects
Dirt/Grass	No effect	No effect	No effect	–
Concrete	No effect	+25%	No effect	-10% to Piloting skill rolls
Rough	No effect	Cannot traverse	No effect	–
Snow	-5%	-75% top speed	-50%	–
Thick Underbrush	No effect	Cannot traverse	No effect	–
Shallow Water	No effect	Cannot traverse	Cannot traverse	Heat sink efficiency=150%; -10% to Piloting skill rolls
Mid-Water	-40% at the deepest; the deeper the water, the more 'Mechs are slowed	Cannot traverse	Cannot traverse	Heat sink efficiency=200%; -20% to Piloting skill rolls
Oceanic Depths	Cannot traverse	Cannot traverse	Cannot traverse	–
Flat Swamp	No effect	Cannot traverse	Cannot traverse	–
Thick Swamp	No effect unless the 'Mech is in water	Cannot traverse	Cannot traverse	–

Combat Strategies

Obviously, the goal in combat is to inflict as much damage as possible upon your enemy as quickly as you can. In other words, you need to kill him before he kills you. The following sections give you some vital information on how to do just that.

Grouping Weapons

Most offensive strategies are about hitting your targets hard and fast. One of the best ways to deliver the maximum amount of damage per shot is to fire your weapons in groups rather than individually (see Figure 2.1).

A 'Mech can have up to six weapon groups, each of which is assigned to a different trigger. You can put any number of weapons in each group. By default, *MechWarrior 4* groups weapons as shown in Table 2.2.

Properly grouped weapons mean a more potent 'Mech.

Table 2.2: Default Weapon Groups

Group	Weapons
1	Instantaneous direct-fire weapons
2	Guided missiles
3	Noninstantaneous direct-fire weapons
4	NARC Beacon
5	Long Tom
6	Artillery

Even though you're allowed to mix and match weapon types in any group you want to set up, certain ones will always work best together. As a general rule, range and speed should determine how they are grouped. For the first three weapon groups, which usually comprise your primary armament, the optimum strategy is as follows:

▸ Group one should consist of fast and/or short-range weaponry. These are the primary weapons that you'll fire most often.

⊂▷ Group two works well as a missile-only group.

⊂▷ Group three should include your most powerful weapons—the ones that have a long recycle time but really pack a wallop.

By grouping your weapons logically, you always know which will be ready the fastest. Separating them by type also keeps the targeting characteristics similar for all the weapons in a group. For example, were you to include lasers and a Long Tom in the same weapon group, you would never be able to hit your target with both weapons at once—their aiming mechanisms are completely different. Finally, by keeping the range of the weapons in a given group fairly close, you can be assured that when the enemy is within range of one weapon, *all* of the weapons in that group will be able to hit him.

> TIP
>
> Although you can set up six weapon groups, three is actually the optimum number. By default, the controls for groups one through three are mapped directly to joystick buttons, while groups four through six require you to hold the Shift key down when firing. Also, the more groups you have, the fewer number of weapons each contains. Fewer weapons makes the group less powerful.

Selective Targeting

By design, 'Mechs are very difficult to destroy. They are heavily armored from head to toe, and are made to withstand a great deal of punishment. So, you may ask, how does one go about destroying these things?

That's not an easy question to answer, as you'll face many different varieties of BattleMechs over the course of the game. There are, however, three ways to destroy an enemy 'Mech:

> TIP
>
> The easiest way to target specific body parts is to remain at medium range and use the zoom reticle to aim your shots. When in zoom mode, use small control movements to keep the target in your sights. If you lose sight of the enemy, turn off the zoom and reorient yourself rather than attempting to reacquire it in the zoomed view.

⊂▷ Destroy its head

⊂▷ Destroy its center torso

⊂▷ Destroy both legs

Hitting these sections isn't particularly easy even under the best conditions—but it's even more difficult to accomplish if you fire haphazardly, scattering your shots all over the target's body. The answer to this dilemma is careful, selective targeting.

Instead of firing wildly, take your time and line up your shots so that they hit the target 'Mech in precise locations (see Figure 2.2). The center torso is the most heavily armored and, therefore, takes the longest time to destroy. The head, while comparatively weak, is difficult to hit. That leaves the legs as the best target for the kill. Even though the legs are heavily armored and you must destroy *both*

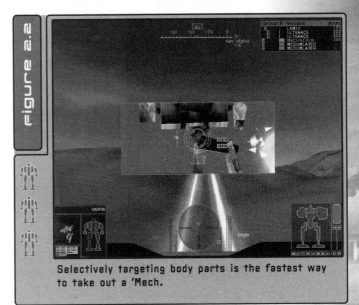

Selectively targeting body parts is the fastest way to take out a 'Mech.

of them in order to destroy the target, they are relatively easy to hit. Also, damaging the legs slows the 'Mech down, making every ensuing shot a little easier to aim.

Finding the Optimum Combat Range

Survival, especially in a 'Mech vs. 'Mech battle, often depends on finding and maintaining your optimum combat range. To hone this skill, you need experience—and a lot of it! There are, however, some things you can do prior to entering a battle that will help determine what range works best for you.

Study your 'Mech. Knowing your 'Mech's weapon loadout, speed, and handling characteristics before you jump into the cockpit is the best way to determine the most effective fighting style. The distance you can shoot and the amount of punishment your armor can sustain are the primary considerations when it comes to range. Refer to Chapter 3: BattleMechs and Non-'Mech Vehicles and Chapter 4: Weapons and Components for more on this topic.

Study other 'Mechs. Know what your opponent's BattleMech is capable of before going into a battle. Your vehicle might be good in a brawl, but your opponent's weapons might be more powerful or have greater range. If you familiarize yourself with all of the 'Mechs and their standard loadouts, you'll know exactly what you're up against the moment you lock onto your target.

Soften up the enemy from a distance. Your 'Mech might excel at short-range combat, but if you have long-range weapons, you might as well take advantage of them. Fire off a few long-range volleys to take some of the fight out of your enemy before closing in. This is especially important when you're dealing with bigger, stronger 'Mechs.

Use hit-and-run tactics. If you don't have any long-range weapons and you're up against a bigger foe, dodge in and out of his weapons range, popping off shots until you take the wind out of him. Then, settle in for the kill.

Keep moving when fighting at short range. It's usually not a good idea to remain close to any 'Mech for a long period of time. Of course, if you're limited to short-range weapons, you don't have much of a choice. When you're close to your enemy, keep moving so you're harder to hit. Travel in a circular pattern around the enemy if possible, keeping your torso (and, thus, your weapons) turned toward him at all times. Keep up a good speed, and your opponent will have a tough time locking onto you.

Special Attack Moves

Most of the combat you'll experience is fairly straightforward. General techniques—such as targeting specific body parts and circling your enemy while twisting your BattleMech's torso to keep him in your sights—are the staples of a good, solid offense. However, certain circumstances call for desperate measures and a healthy dose of innovation. There are also times when you'll get the drop on the bad guys and want to give them something extra-special to remember you by. The following sections describe a few of the more unorthodox offensive moves you can try.

Ramming

One thing emphasized in both the game and this guide is the sheer size of a 'Mech. They're huge, they're tough, and their weapons pack a wallop. They're not fun to run into—literally as well as figuratively!

Ramming your 'Mech into any destructible object in the game damages that object. The amount of damage inflicted depends on both the speed of the 'Mech at the time of the collision and the tonnage of the colliding 'Mech (see Table 2.3).

Table 2.3: Ramming Damage

'Mech Speed (KpH)*	Damage Inflicted (Hit Points)
< 20	2**
20–50	Tonnage/10
51–90	Tonnage/5
91–120	Tonnage/2
>120	Tonnage

*The speed of each 'Mech in a multi-'Mech collision is treated separately.
**Ramming another 'Mech at speeds of less than 20 KpH inflicts no damage.

Ramming any non-'Mech object (buildings, vehicles, and so on) inflicts damage *only* to the object that is rammed. That means that you can step on and run into anything that isn't a 'Mech with impunity and not worry about the consequences. This is a fast and easy way to wade through a convoy of ground vehicles—especially if they're unarmed and can't take potshots at you as you approach (see Figure 2.3).

> **NOTE**
> 'Mechs have eight separate areas that can be damaged in five zones: head, arms, left and right sides of the torso, center torso, and legs. When you ram another 'Mech, the total damage is divided into five equal groups and applied randomly amongst all the body parts struck in the collision.

Ramming other 'Mechs is a different story. When two 'Mechs collide, each deals damage to the other as per Table 2.3. In addition, each 'Mech takes half the damage it dished out upon itself.

Obviously, ramming other 'Mechs should be considered a last-ditch tactic because of the damage you'll sustain in return. However, there are times—like when you're out of ammo or all your weapons are destroyed—when there is no alternative.

Taking out some vehicles the easy way

Setting up an Ambush

One of the limitations of 'Mech sensors is the inability to detect other 'Mechs when they're shut down. In Chapter 1: Taking Control, we mentioned that having your lancemates shut down and lie in wait was a strategy you could use to lure an enemy into a trap.

You don't need to have lancemates with you in order to set up an ambush, though. Another option is to shut down your own 'Mech and lie in wait yourself. This is a simple strategy, but it requires some planning for it to be effective. The key is location. Set yourself up in a place where you won't be visible to the enemy until the last minute (see Figure 2.4). Remember that while you might be off enemy sensors, it's pretty easy to spot a 30-foot-tall BattleMech standing in the middle of an open field. Stay put until your enemy appears, then power up and let him have it with both barrels!

An effective ambush requires a good hiding place.

Something to remember when attempting this trick is that only basic sensors are fooled by it. There's no point in shutting down if your enemies are equipped with Beagle Active Probes—you'll only have that much less time to react when they start pummeling you.

Death from Above

The maneuver called "death from above" (DFA) is, by far, the showiest offensive tactic you can perform (see Figure 2.5). It's difficult to master the timing and control required, but boy, is it fun when you get it right!

To perform this maneuver, you have to be piloting a 'Mech equipped with Jump Jets. Simply (yeah, right)

figure 2.5

Attempting to deal some death from above

locate your target, jump into the air, and land on top of him. If you succeed, you inflict upon your enemy an amount of damage equal to three-fifths of your 'Mech's tonnage (rounded up). For example, if you're in a 50-ton 'Mech, you'll cause 30 points of damage. This damage is then divided into five equal groups (see earlier note for more info) and distributed randomly across the upper body parts of the target 'Mech. Unfortunately, you can't damage the target's legs in a DFA.

> **NOTE**
>
> Both the leg damage and overbalancing problems encountered in a DFA apply only when you're attacking another 'Mech. Performing a DFA against a non-'Mech vehicle causes you no inconvenience whatsoever.

There are negative consequences even when this maneuver is performed success-fully. First, your 'Mech takes damage—one-tenth of your total tonnage (rounded up).

This damage is applied equally to your 'Mech's legs. Also, a DFA causes both 'Mechs to overbalance, which means there's a chance that one (or both) of you could fall.

Despite its difficulty and obvious dangers, the DFA is extremely satisfying when performed successfully. It also comes as a real shock to your enemy, especially in a multiplayer game. Just don't depend on something this tricky as a primary attack maneuver.

Resource Management and Salvage

In *MechWarrior 4*'s campaign, you're fighting on the side of the underdogs. This means your supplies and equipment are quite limited when you start the game. That's the bad news.

The good news is that after just about every mission, there is a chance that enemy equipment left on the battlefield can be picked up as salvage. This is the only way you have of increasing your stockpile of 'Mechs and weapons.

Every campaign mission has a number of specified salvage items that might or might not be available at its conclusion (the specific salvage materiel left over from each mission is discussed in Part 3: Campaign Walkthrough). Some of the items are obtained no matter what, but the availability of others is dependent on your actions.

The most important items you can obtain this way is 'Mech equipment from destroyed enemy 'Mechs. At the end of each mission, there is a percentage chance of salvaging the chassis and components of any 'Mechs you've defeated. It doesn't matter how you kill enemy 'Mechs; just destroy as many as you can to improve your salvage chances (see Figure 2.6).

Destroy a 'Mech to increase your salvage.

part 2

mechs,
vehicles, and
weapons

*P*art 2 of this guide introduces you to the hardware you'll be dealing with in MechWarrior 4: Vengeance. First and foremost, you'll learn about the 'Mechs themselves. These towering war machines, the most deadly ever designed by man, come in a variety of shapes and sizes. You need to understand the operational details of each of the 21 'Mechs in the game to fully comprehend what your own vehicle is capable of—and what the enemy's 'Mech can do to you. We'll even give you some tips on how to improve upon the game's default 'Mech designs by dabbling in the MechLab.

Since 'Mechs aren't the only enemies you'll have to deal with, we'll also provide all the information you need on the other vehicles you'll encounter on the battlefield. The section is completed with full details on the weapons and components that make 'Mechs such fearsome instruments of destruction. We'll show you every devastating device you have available and give you the lowdown on which weapons work best in any given combat situation.

So, read on and discover the vast arsenal of equipment you have at your disposal in MechWarrior 4.

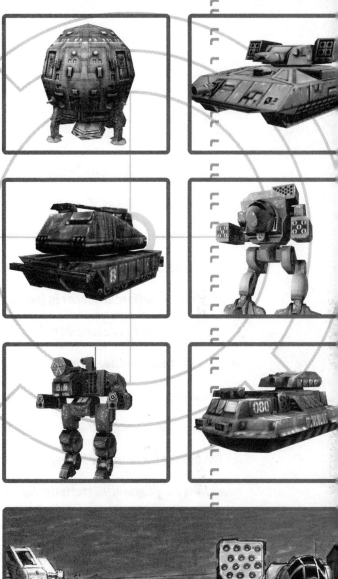

chapter 3

Battlemechs and Non-'mech Vehicles

One of the best ways to excel at MechWarrior 4: Vengeance is to become familiar with the BattleMechs themselves. Knowing the ins and outs of every 'Mech not only makes you better at controlling your own war machine—it makes you aware of what you're up against in battle.

A total of 21 different 'Mechs is included in the game—12 from the Inner Sphere and 9 from the Clan. Each is described in full detail in this chapter. Many of these are classic designs that are familiar fixtures in the MechWarrior universe. However, six Inner Sphere designs and one Clan design are new to this game. So even seasoned 'Mech combat veterans will benefit from a look through the pages that follow.

The bulk of this chapter is devoted to the 'Mechs themselves. Individual entries reveal not only their vital statistics but also general strategies on how to both operate and defeat them. Once you've read this section, you'll know the strengths and capabilities inherent in your own war machine, and will be able to take advantage of the weaknesses and flaws of those used by your enemies. We'll also take a look at how to customize your rides with the MechLab. Building a better 'Mech has never been so easy.

In the remainder of the chapter, we'll take a brief look at the other vehicles you might encounter on the battlefield. Even though these tend to be less dangerous than enemy 'Mechs, it's still helpful to know what's nipping at your heels while you're trying to accomplish your mission objectives.

BattleMech Vital Statistics

BattleMechs are complex machines, and as such have many vital statistics. For ease of reference, we've divided them into several categories:

Basic Statistics: This section includes the general stats for each 'Mech, including origin (Inner Sphere or Clan), weight, armor type, and speed. This information is included with each individual description and in Table 3.22.

Loadout: The default weapons and equipment carried by the BattleMech. A table showing this information appears along with the description of each 'Mech (weapons are described in detail in Chapter 4: Weapons and Components).

Hit Point Breakdown: Armor and internal structure Hit Points of each 'Mech, broken down by body part. Full details appear in Table 3.23.

Tonnage Breakdown: A breakdown of each 'Mech's overall tonnage into its component parts. A complete list including all 'Mech types can be found in Table 3.24.

Please note that the specifications in this chapter apply to each 'Mech's default loadout and configuration. You can, of course, make changes to your 'Mech in the MechLab.

A BattleMech's performance characteristics and battlefield role

NOTE

One of the features included in *MechWarrior 4* is the MechLab, a design tool that lets you change the weapons loadout and certain design features of your BattleMech before going into battle. It's important to remember that any changes you make to the vehicle's configuration alter the base statistics shown in this chapter (the MechLab itself is discussed later in this chapter).

NOTE

The seven new 'Mechs in *MechWarrior 4* are the Osiris (light 'Mech); Chimera, Hellspawn, Uziel, and Argus (medium 'Mechs); Thanatos (heavy 'Mech); and Mad Cat MK. II (assault 'Mech).

are primarily determined by its weight. All 'Mechs in *MechWarrior 4* fall into one of the following weight classes:

- **Light:** 20–35 tons
- **Medium:** 36–55 tons
- **Heavy:** 56–75 tons
- **Assault:** 76–100 tons

This chapter groups Inner Sphere and Clan 'Mechs by maximum tonnage in each weight category for easy comparison.

TIP

When you're at the helm of a light 'Mech, the best general strategy is to keep moving. Use your speed to evade incoming fire rather than relying on your armor to absorb it.

Light 'Mechs

Light BattleMechs are designed for speed and agility rather than firepower and endurance. Though some are quite capable of holding their own in a prolonged firefight with other 'Mechs of their size or even larger, they simply lack enough armor to give them much of a chance against their larger counterparts.

Osiris (New)

Chassis Tech Type	Inner Sphere
Maximum Tonnage	30
Armor Type	Ferro-Fibrous
Top Speed (KpH)	130

The Osiris is the lightest 'Mech in the game. At the same time, it is also one dangerous little war machine. Its speed tops that of the next fastest 'Mech by a significant amount, and the Osiris' incredible maneuverability makes its relatively thin armor a negligible drawback.

TIP

The key to defeating an Osiris is long-range attacks. The last thing you want to do is get into a face-to-face brawl with a 'Mech this fast—you won't get a shot in edgewise.

Although it lacks the long-range capabilities of the other light 'Mechs, the Osiris' impressive combination of lasers and ballistic weapons makes it quite potent at medium and short range. It lacks the overall punch of the Cougar but, by using its speed and maneuverability to stay out of the way of incoming fire, the Osiris can be just as deadly in the long run.

Table 3.1: Osiris Default Loadout

Weapon/Component	Location	Total Weight (Tons)
SRM6	Left Arm	4
Medium Laser (5)	Center Torso (Special 2) (2), Right Arm (2), Right Torso (Special 1)	5
Machine Gun Array	Right Torso (Special 1)	2

Raven

Chassis Tech Type	Inner Sphere
Maximum Tonnage	35
Armor Type	Ferro-Fibrous
Top Speed (KpH)	100

At first glance, the Raven seems to be the least formidable of the light 'Mechs. It is strictly middle of the road when it comes to speed, and in its standard configuration, both the Osiris and the Cougar outgun it at close range. However, there's more to the Raven than meets the eye.

Designed primarily as an electronic warfare platform, the Raven's major strength lies in its extensive electronics package. A Beagle Active Probe, a Guardian ECM, and a NARC Beacon are all standard issue on this 'Mech. When it comes to light, long-range attack vehicles, the Raven is among the best. While it isn't terribly difficult to take on the stock version of this 'Mech at close range, it is always a force to be reckoned with from a distance.

Unlike the other two light 'Mechs, the Raven is not Jump Jet capable.

TABLE 3.2: RAVEN DEFAULT LOADOUT

Weapon/Component	Location	Total Weight (Tons)
NARC Beacon	Left Arm	3
Small Pulse Laser (2)	Right Arm, Right Torso	2
Small Laser	Right Torso	0.5
LRM15	Right Torso	8

Cougar

Chassis Tech Type	Clan
Maximum Tonnage	35
Armor Type	Ferro-Fibrous
Top Speed (KpH)	97

In terms of armor protection, the Cougar is in the same league as the other two light 'Mechs. Its default weapons package, however, is much more diverse than that of both the Osiris and the Raven. And the added range and damage potential of its Clan weaponry give it an edge over its cousins at any given range. The Cougar's mix of weapons allows it to soften up enemies at long range before moving in to finish them off. This strategy allows this 'Mech to effectively engage larger foes than would normally be possible for such a light 'Mech.

Strangely enough, the one slight weakness of the Cougar is its speed. This is the slowest of the three light 'Mechs. It actually falls into the performance parameters of significantly heavier Clan 'Mechs. Even so, this weakness is minor. The opposing combatant will need to be very skilled to exploit it.

INFO

Clan 'Mechs are, as a general rule, superior to their Inner Sphere counterparts. They tend to carry more weapons and armor for their size while still besting Inner Sphere 'Mechs of similar weight in terms of speed. Also, Clan 'Mechs are naturally equipped with Clan weapons, which, as discussed in Chapter 4: Weapons and Components, are more effective than their Inner Sphere counterparts.

Table 3.3: Cougar Default Loadout

Weapon/Component	Location	Total Weight (Tons)
Clan ER Small Laser	Left Arm	0.5
Clan ER Medium Laser	Left Arm	1
Clan ER Large Laser (2)	Left Arm, Right Arm	8
Clan LRM10 (2)	Left Torso, Right Torso	7

Medium 'Mechs

Medium BattleMechs are a compromise between the bristling weapons and thick armor of the heavy class and the speed and agility of the light. While this thicker skin makes it possible for these 'Mechs to withstand a bit more punishment than their lighter brethren, their movement and evasion capabilities are still very much the key to survival in prolonged encounters.

Chimera (New)

Chassis Tech Type	Inner Sphere
Maximum Tonnage	40
Armor Type	Laser Reflective
Top Speed (KpH)	102

As the lightest of the medium 'Mechs, the Chimera has offensive performance and handling characteristics very much like those of its light 'Mech counterparts. Its armor has a slight edge over that of the light 'Mechs, but not enough to make it stand out.

The Chimera's default weapons mix is best suited to medium-range attacks. It falls short of all the light 'Mechs when it comes to short-range combat performance, and it has no real long-range weaponry to speak of. Because of its larger

Chimeras are equipped with Laser Reflective Armor, which greatly reduces the effectiveness of beam weapon attacks. When you're up against them—or any other 'Mech sheathed in this armor type—make projectiles and missiles your weapons of choice.

size, this 'Mech is capable of carrying more firepower, though both speed and armor would suffer as a result. Even so, the Chimera could definitely benefit from a better weapons package.

Table 3.4: Chimera Default Loadout

Weapon/Component	Location	Total Weight (Tons)
Large Laser	Left Arm	5
Medium Laser	Left Arm	1
MRM20	Right Torso	8
Machine Gun Array	Right Arm	2

Hellspawn (New)

Chassis Tech Type	Inner Sphere
Maximum Tonnage	45
Armor Type	Ferro-Fibrous
Top Speed (KpH)	106

The Hellspawn is one of the most versatile 'Mechs in its size class. Its two long-range missile racks make it an excellent fire-support vehicle. Unlike many 'Mechs designed exclusively for such a role, however, the Hellspawn also shines in medium- to close-range combat. With a top speed that exceeds every other 'Mech in its class (and some of the smaller 'Mechs as well), the Hellspawn is a highly maneuverable brawler. It packs enough firepower to do some serious damage.

The best strategy to adopt when opposing this powerful machine is to hit it hard from beyond the range of its lasers. Most 'Mechs of like or larger size will have a tough time keeping the Hellspawn in their sights at close range.

Table 3.5: Hellspawn Default Loadout

Weapon/Component	Location	Total Weight (Tons)
Medium Pulse Laser (3)	Left Arm, Right Arm, Right Torso	6
LRM10 (2)	Left Torso, Right Arm (Special 1)	12

Uziel (New)

Chassis Tech Type	Inner Sphere
Maximum Tonnage	50
Armor Type	Ferro-Fibrous
Top Speed (KpH)	95

When properly controlled, the Uziel can be a reasonably effective short- to medium-range 'Mech. Its speed and maneuverability allow it to keep up with lighter rivals, and it has the armor to absorb a few hits when evasion isn't an option.

The main offensive power of this 'Mech comes from its twin Particle Projection Cannons (PPCs). While these weapons are extremely potent and can shred targets at both short and medium range, they produce a *lot* of heat. That makes the Uziel prone to overheating problems if handled incorrectly. For this reason, the Uziel must use its speed and agility to launch hit-and-fade attacks, using the PPCs judiciously and allowing their heat to dissipate before firing again. Overheating is likely to get the best of this 'Mech if it's forced into a prolonged toe-to-toe brawl.

Table 3.6: Uziel Default Loadout

Weapon/Component	Location	Total Weight (Tons)
PPC (2)	Left Arm, Right Arm	14
Machine Gun Array (2)	Left Torso, Right Torso	3
SRM6	Center Torso (Special 1)	4

Bushwacker

Chassis Tech Type	Inner Sphere
Maximum Tonnage	55
Armor Type	Ferro-Fibrous
Top Speed (KpH)	85

The Bushwacker is a middle-of-the-road medium 'Mech and it performs like one. It is armored and armed in the style of a typical medium design, but its speed and performance parameters are more in line with those of heavier 'Mechs.

Bushwackers are equipped with a standard weapons package that makes them capable of engaging in combat at any distance. From a strictly offensive standpoint, this 'Mech is definitely superior to the smaller Inner Sphere medium designs. Its lack of agility and Jump Jets do make it difficult for the Bushwacker to move out of the way when things get too hot for the armor to handle. For this reason, its best role is that of long-range fire support and attack.

Table 3.7: Bushwacker Default Loadout

Weapon/Component	Location	Total Weight (Tons)
LRM5	Left Arm	3
LRM10	Left Torso (Special 1)	6
AC10	Right Arm	7
Medium Pulse Laser (2)	Center Torso	4

Shadow Cat

Chassis Tech Type	Clan
Maximum Tonnage	45
Armor Type	Ferro-Fibrous
Top Speed (KpH)	102

The Shadow Cat once again shows the inherent advantages of Clan 'Mechs over those of the Inner Sphere. Though it has far more firepower than Inner Sphere designs of similar weight, the Shadow Cat's speed and performance rival those of much lighter 'Mechs.

In their standard configuration, Shadow Cats are geared primarily toward short- and medium-range combat. It is as nimble as a much lighter 'Mech. This gives it enough maneuverability to hold its own for quite some time, avoiding damage by using its superior speed and its Jump Jets to stay out of harm's way. As with all Clan 'Mechs, its Clan-designed weapons give it an edge over similarly armed Inner Sphere 'Mechs when it comes to range and damage potential.

This 'Mech's main flaw is its lack of significant long-range firepower. Most of its weapons are useless beyond 400 meters. It is this deficiency that makes the Shadow Cat's close combat abilities so important. Any opponent with sufficient long-range weaponry that can manage to keep its distance is a serious threat to the Shadow Cat.

Table 3.8: Shadow Cat Default Loadout

Weapon/Component	Location	Total Weight (Tons)
Clan ER Large Laser Left Arm	4	
Clan ER Med. Pulse Laser (3)	Right Arm (2), Right Torso	6
Clan ER Small Laser	Right Torso	0.5
Clan Machine Gun Array (2)	Right Torso	3
STRK6	Left Torso	4

Heavy 'Mechs

When you start driving heavy BattleMechs, the need for speed decreases somewhat. Even though many heavy 'Mechs are capable of significant speeds—especially Clan designs—they can generally stand their ground in a fight because of liberal amounts of thick armor. Fighting in and against heavy 'Mechs is more about delivering and absorbing damage than avoiding it.

Argus [New]

Chassis Tech Type	Inner Sphere
Maximum Tonnage	60
Armor Type	Laser Reflective
Top Speed (KpH)	81

Inner Sphere medium 'Mechs don't come any heavier than the Argus. Its thick Laser Reflective Armor is particularly adept at repelling attacks from Clan 'Mechs of the same class, which tend to have beam-intensive loadouts. This defensive edge makes it an excellent bet to survive a battle against its peers.

The default weapons mix has something for every combat range, though it excels in medium- to short-range confrontations. One potential offensive flaw is that most of the Argus' armament is ammunition-intensive. While ballistic weapons and missiles pack a lot of punch, prolonged battles can render 'Mechs that carry them into nothing but an armored shell with lots of empty guns and launchers. Even though the Argus carries some beam weapons as well, most of its teeth are gone once the ballistic ammo and missiles run out.

Table 3.9: Argus Default Loadout

Weapon/Component	Location	Total Weight (Tons)
LRM10	Left Arm	6
Medium Laser (2)	Left Torso, Right Torso	2
Ultra AC5 (2)	Right Arm	19
Machine Gun Array	Right Arm	2

Catapult

Chassis Tech Type	Inner Sphere
Maximum Tonnage	65
Armor Type	Reactive
Top Speed (KpH)	76

The Catapult is a 'Mech that lives up to its name, being clearly designed to hurl projectiles from a distance. This heavy 'Mech is clearly designed to fill the role of a long-range attack vehicle. This 'Mech's default loadout includes two racks of powerful long-range missiles and Reactive Armor. As long as a Catapult manages to maintain its distance from its opponents, it is an extremely difficult machine to deal with.

Like all large 'Mechs, the Catapult is more than up to the challenge of surviving a prolonged confrontation. However, the design of the vehicle (which lacks the manipulative, multi-purpose arms common to most heavy 'Mechs) and its weapons loadout make it poorly suited for close-range combat. Though its lasers can do quite a bit of damage in a brawl, they are ultimately no match for the powerful weapons mix of other 'Mechs in this class.

> A heavy 'Mech equipped with Jump Jets is ideal for the "death from above" tactic (for more, see the "Special Attack Moves" section of Chapter 2: Combat Tactics 101). Jumping into the air and landing on an opponent inflicts a devastating amount of damage.

Table 3.10: Catapult Default Loadout

Weapon/Component	Location	Total Weight (Tons)
Small Pulse Laser	Center Torso	1
LRM20 (2)	Left Arm, Right Arm	22
Large Laser	Right Torso	5

Thanatos (New)

Chassis Tech Type	Inner Sphere
Maximum Tonnage	75
Armor Type	Ferro-Fibrous
Top Speed (KpH)	81

You'd be hard pressed to find a 'Mech better suited to medium-range combat than the Thanatos. A battery of Medium Pulse Lasers backs up a powerful LBX-AC20 and a rack of MRM20 missiles. This deadly combination is guaranteed to shred enemies in the 300- to 400-meter range.

The Thanatos' top speed is on par with other 'Mechs of similar weight, and its armor is more than sufficient to protect it in prolonged battles. Rounding out its impressive equipment loadout is a Guardian ECM system. This 'Mech's only flaw is its total lack of long-range weaponry. If an opponent with long-range capability manages to spot the Thanatos before it can close to its own combat range, the enemy 'Mech can inflict serious damage before the Thanatos can bring its own weapons to bear.

ECM is an important component in the Thanatos design, as it increases the 'Mech's chances of closing to effective range before it is spotted by the enemy. Just remember that ECM also increases the enemy's missile lock capabilities.

Table 3.11: Thanatos Default Loadout

Weapon/Component	Location	Total Weight (Tons)
LBX-AC20	Left Arm	15
Medium Pulse Laser (4)	Left Arm (2), Left Torso (2)	8
MRM20	Right Arm	8

Vulture

Chassis Tech Type	Clan
Maximum Tonnage	60
Armor Type	Reactive
Top Speed (KpH)	85

A stock Vulture is the exact opposite of a Shadow Cat when it comes to combat range. As the heavier of the two Clan medium 'Mechs, it is primarily a long-range attacker. Its battery of LRM20s and Large Pulse Lasers is great at carving up targets from a significant distance.

Of course, this is not to say that Vultures are incapable of holding their own in an all-out brawl. The short-range weaponry of this 'Mech packs quite a punch, and its speed is slightly better than average for its weight. All things considered, Vultures are arguably the most diverse and deadly medium class 'Mechs in the game.

> One factor that makes the Vulture effective as a long-range combatant is its Reactive Armor. This plating significantly decreases the effectiveness of long-range projectile and missile attacks. Make beams your weapons of choice any time you're up against an enemy with Reactive Armor.

Table 3.12: Vulture Default Loadout

Weapon/Component	Location	Total Weight (Tons)
Clan ER Large Pulse Laser (2)	Left Arm, Right Arm	12
Clan LRM20 (2)	Left Torso, Right Torso	12
Clan ER Med. Pulse Laser (2)	Center Torso (Special 1)	4

Loki

Chassis Tech Type	Clan
Maximum Tonnage	65
Armor Type	Ferro-Fibrous
Top Speed (KpH)	83

As is typical of Clan 'Mechs, the Loki is more than capable of matching much larger 'Mechs in a head-to-head battle and coming out on top. The usual performance factors—superior speed and a deadly weapons loadout (which is unusually potent for its size)—are responsible for this Clan 'Mech's superiority.

In its default configuration, the Loki is useless at long range. If you're up against one in combat, keeping your distance is the best key to victory. If you're in the cockpit of an unmodified Loki, use your 'Mech the way that it was meant to be used: wade right in and start brawling. Use your ECM to sneak into optimum firing range before the enemy spots you.

Table 3.13: Loki Default Loadout

Weapon/Component	Location	Total Weight (Tons)
Clan ER Med. Pulse Laser (2)	Left Arm, Right Arm	4
Clan ER Med. Laser (2)	Left Arm, Right Arm	2
Clan LBX-AC10 (2)	Left Arm, Right Arm	20
Clan LAMS	Left Torso	1.5
STRK6	Right Torso (Special 1)	4

Nova Cat

Chassis Tech Type	Clan
Maximum Tonnage	70
Armor Type	Laser Reflective
Top Speed (KpH)	73

Nova Cats are unusually slow for Clan heavy 'Mechs. In fact, they are by far the slowest of this class, their maximum speed falling below even the Inner Sphere large 'Mechs.

But don't let that lull you into a sense of complacency. The Nova Cat makes up for this minor shortcoming by packing a punch that is more than a match for any other heavy 'Mech. Every weapon on board is a beam weapon with the range and power to make the Nova Cat a formidable opponent at any range. The design includes Laser Reflective Armor, so the Nova Cat is also well equipped to take the same sort of damage it dishes out.

If you find yourself up against a Nova Cat, your best bet is to keep moving and stay out of its line of fire. This is about the only Clan 'Mech that is usually at a *dis-advantage* when it comes to speed. Also try to keep your distance as much as possible. Attack from long range with missiles and projectiles unless you're certain of a quick kill.

As with any PPC-laden 'Mech, over-heating is an ever-looming problem. Care must be taken to give the heat sinks time to cool things down between shots.

Table 3.14: Nova Cat Default Loadout

Weapon/Component	Location	Total Weight (Tons)
Clan ER Large Laser (3)	Left Arm	12
Clan ER Small Pulse Laser	Left Torso	1.5
Clan ER PPC (2)	Right Arm	12

Thor

Chassis Tech Type	Clan
Maximum Tonnage	70
Armor Type	Ferro-Fibrous
Top Speed (KpH)	85

The Thor is much more typical of Clan heavy 'Mechs than the Nova Cat. The ability of Clan heavy 'Mechs to perform with the speed and agility of their much lighter counterparts makes them a force to be reckoned with.

Of course, there's more to the Thor than speed. Its standard weapons package provides a great deal of short- to medium-range firepower. Only the more heavily armed (and equally fast) Mad Cat is a more dangerous heavy 'Mech to go toe-to-toe with. Your best bet if you're up against a Thor is to keep your distance and hope that your long-range armament can take charge of the situation before a tactical battle becomes a brawl.

Table 3.15: Thor Default Loadout

Weapon/Component	Location	Total Weight (Tons)
Clan Ultra AC5 (2)	Left Arm, Right Arm	16
Clan ER Small Laser (4)	Left Arm, Right Arm, Right Torso (2)	2
Clan LRM15	Left Torso (Special 1)	4.5
Clan Machine Gun Array	Right Torso	2

Mad Cat

Chassis Tech Type	Clan
Maximum Tonnage	75
Armor Type	Ferro-Fibrous
Top Speed (KpH)	85

When it comes to heavy 'Mechs, the Mad Cat is the undisputed all-around champion. No other BattleMech in this class packs the versatility of firepower found in this beast. Add to that a speed that rivals 'Mechs almost half the Mad Cat's weight, and you get a war machine that you just don't want to mess with. So what if it doesn't have quite as much armor as some of the others in its class? Opponents likely won't be around long enough to find that out.

There is little that the Mad Cat cannot do. In its default configuration, it has teeth at all ranges, from short to long. Its superior speed enables it to run circles around any opponent in its class, tearing the other 'Mech to shreds and taking just about anything a foe can dish out.

TIP

The center torso of the Mad Cat is huge. Aim for this specific location, and you will eventually punch through. Now your only problem is doing this without being destroyed by the Mad Cat first.

Table 3.16: Mad Cat Default Loadout

Weapon/Component	Location	Total Weight (Tons)
Clan ER Large Laser (2)	Left Arm, Right Arm	8
Clan ER Med. Laser (2)	Left Arm, Right Arm	2
Clan LRM20 (2)	Left Torso (Special 1), Right Torso (Special 2)	12
Clan ER Med. Pulse Laser (2)	Left Torso, Right Torso	4
Clan Machine Gun Array (2)	Left Torso, Right Torso	3

Assault 'Mechs

There is no BattleMech in the game more impressive than the largest of the lot: the assault 'Mechs. These behemoths weigh in at up to 100 tons, and pack enough firepower to lay waste to a small city. They're slow and lack maneuverability, but they make up for their inability to dodge incoming fire with enough armor to take nearly everything that the opposition can throw at them.

When given a choice, it's always tempting to grab the assault 'Mech. Just keep one thing in mind: destruction is lots of fun, but a few skillful opponents in smaller, quicker 'Mechs can take advantage of your lack of maneuverability and bring you down. And remember that everybody likes to pick on the assault 'Mech in multiplayer games.

By their very nature, assault 'Mechs are geared toward medium- to long-range combat. In a short-range conflict, they lack the maneuverability and speed to track faster targets. This is their primary flaw, and it can be capitalized upon should a more maneuverable enemy manage to get close enough.

Awesome

Chassis Tech Type	Inner Sphere
Maximum Tonnage	80
Armor Type	Ferro-Fibrous
Top Speed (KpH)	75

The Awesome has long been one of the favorite 'Mechs of the Inner Sphere—and with good reason. Although it isn't capable of the speeds reached by the lighter Thanatos, the Awesome more than makes up for that deficit in its armor and armaments.

This 'Mech is ideal for short- to medium-range combat. Its default loadout is perfect for the large 'Mech class—it's designed to quickly shred one opponent and move on to the next. This firepower comes at a potential cost, however. Its dependency on PPCs makes overheating a constantly looming threat. Care must be exercised to avoid overtaxing the heat sinks in a prolonged confrontation.

Table 3.17: Awesome Default Loadout

Weapon/Component	Location	Total Weight (Tons)
SRM2 (2)	Center Torso	3
PPC (3)	Left Torso, Right Arm, Right Torso	21
Medium Pulse Laser (2)	Left Arm	4

Mauler

Chassis Tech Type	Inner Sphere
Maximum Tonnage	90
Armor Type	Reactive
Top Speed (KpH)	65

The Mauler is definitely one of the more impressive-looking 'Mechs in the game. Under the right circumstances, one can see how it got its name. As a long-range attack platform, the Mauler really packs a punch with its missiles and Autocannons. In medium-range combat, its battery of lasers form a potent combination with the multipurpose Autocannons.

This 'Mech's default configuration has two main weaknesses. First, its long-range attack capabilities are fully dependent on weapons that require ammunition. Even though the default loadout includes extra ammo for both the

Autocannons and the missile batteries, there is the potential to run dry in a lengthy confrontation. Therefore, each shot must be planned with great care.

Slow turning speed is this 'Mech's other weakness. This makes it easy for an enemy at long range to avoid the Mauler's Autocannon fire. The more distant the target, the easier it is for them to move out of the way. Since the Autocannons are an important component of the Mauler's long-range attack capability, this is a grave weakness indeed.

> Because they can carry so many weapons, assault 'Mechs commonly encounter problems with overheating. If you decide to make any design changes to assault 'Mechs in the MechLab, account for this by including a sufficient number of heat sinks.

Table 3.18: Mauler Default Loadout

Weapon/Component	Location	Total Weight (Tons)
Medium Laser (4)	Left Arm (2), Right Arm (2)	4
Ultra AC2 (4)	Left Torso (2), Right Torso (2)	30
LRM10 (2)	Left Torso, Right Torso	12

Atlas

Chassis Tech Type	Inner Sphere
Maximum Tonnage	100
Armor Type	Ferro-Fibrous
Top Speed (KpH)	57

Befitting the heaviest of the Inner Sphere 'Mechs, the Atlas carries a huge arsenal of weapons. Unlike the Mauler, which is clearly outfitted for long-range assault, the Atlas carries a default weapons loadout that makes it best suited for medium-range combat.

The greatest weakness of the Atlas' default configuration is the surprising number of short-range weapons it carries. Like any assault 'Mech, this one can take a great deal of punishment because of its thick armor (the thickest of all 'Mechs)—but its ponderous speed makes it a sitting duck at short range. Of all the 'Mechs in the game, this is the one that could benefit most from a refit in the MechLab. Replacing the Small Lasers with weapons that have more range will enable the Atlas to become a more formidable opponent at the ranges where it operates best.

Table 3.19: Atlas Default Loadout

Weapon/Component	Location	Total Weight (Tons)
Small Laser	Center Torso	0.5
Medium Laser	Center Torso	1
Small Pulse Laser	Head	1
AMS	Left Arm	0.5
PPC (2)	Left Arm, Right Arm	14
LRM10 (2)	Left Torso, Right Torso	12
Gauss Rifle	Right Torso (Special 1)	16

Mad Cat MK. II (New)

Chassis Tech Type	Clan
Maximum Tonnage	90
Armor Type	Ferro-Fibrous
Top Speed (KpH)	73

The Mad Cat MK. II is the kind of nightmare 'Mech that Clan forces are famous for. This is an assault 'Mech in every sense when it comes to defensive strength and offensive power, but it has performance characteristics that are more in line with a much smaller vehicle. The Mad Cat MK. II is, by far, the fastest in its class. This gives it uncommon agility for its size. It is also the only assault 'Mech with Jump Jets—and this is not the kind of 'Mech you want dropping out of the sky in front of (or on top of!) you.

The weapons loadout is mostly typical of the assault 'Mech class. Its two missile racks rain death from long distance, while two powerful Clan Gauss Rifles are ready for those targets that are slightly

TIP

If you find yourself up against a Mad Cat MK. II, try to stay out of range of its Gauss Rifles. The range and power of these weapons make them among the most dangerous in the game.

closer. Topping off the mix are two pairs of lasers for medium- and short-range fire support.

Target tracking and maneuvering at close ranges is another specialty of the Mad Cat MK. II. It's better in both areas than others in its class, so smaller 'Mechs at short range don't have as much of an advantage as they would against other assault 'Mechs.

TABLE 3.20: MAD CAT MK. II DEFAULT LOADOUT

Weapon/Component	Location	Total Weight (Tons)
Clan Gauss Rifle (2)	Left Arm, Right Arm	26
Clan LRM10 (2)	Left Torso (Special 2), Right Torso (Special 1)	7
Clan ER Med. Laser (4)	Left Torso (2), Right Torso (2)	4

Daishi

Chassis Tech Type	Clan
Maximum Tonnage	100
Armor Type	Ferro-Fibrous
Top Speed (KpH)	51

"Great death"—that's what the name of this assault 'Mech means, and boy does the Daishi ever live up to its designation. This is, hands down, the most lethal piece of hardware in the game. Though it has slightly less armor and is slower than the Inner Sphere's Atlas, the Daishi's default loadout is a textbook example of an effective assault 'Mech. The weapons package is about equally balanced between long- and medium-range armament, most of which are beam weapons (thus requiring no extra tonnage for spare ammunition).

The design also includes a couple of short-range weapons. These, in conjunction with the Daishi's battery of lasers, are enough to shred any enemy that manages to get close. Of course, as

You're in good shape if you find yourself up against a Daishi in a 'Mech that has LRMs as part of its arsenal. Most of the Daishi's long-range firepower is limited to about 800 meters. Keep your distance, and you might be able to take out the Daishi before its single missile battery can destroy you.

with all 'Mechs of this class, the Daishi suffers from sluggish performance that makes short-range combat potentially dangerous in prolonged doses. With an arsenal like this one, however, all it takes is one or two solid shots to destroy an enemy foolish enough to go toe to toe with this behemoth.

Table 3.21: Daishi Default Loadout

Weapon/Component	Location	Total Weight (Tons)
Clan ER Med. Pulse Laser (4)	Center Torso	8
Clan ER Large Laser (4)	Left Arm (2), Right Arm (2)	16
Clan Ultra AC5 (2)	Left Torso, Right Torso	16
Clan Machine Gun Array (2)	Left Torso, Right Torso	4
Clan LRM10	Left Torso (Special 1)	3.5

BattleMech Statistics at a Glance

Table 3.22 shows the basic statistics for all BattleMechs in the game.

Table 3.22: 'Mech Comparison Table

'Mech	Class	Chassis Tech Type	Max Tonnage	Armor Type	Top Speed (KpH)	Jump Jets
Osiris	Light	IS	30	FF	130	Yes
Raven	Light	IS	35	FF	100	No
Cougar	Light	Clan	35	FF	97	Yes
Chimera	Medium	IS	40	Laser Ref.	102	Yes
Hellspawn	Medium	IS	45	FF	106	Yes
Uziel	Medium	IS	50	FF	95	Yes
Bushwacker	Medium	IS	55	FF	85	No
Shadow Cat	Medium	Clan	45	FF	102	Yes
Argus	Heavy	IS	60	Laser Ref.	81	No
Catapult	Heavy	IS	65	Reactive	76	Yes
Thanatos	Heavy	IS	75	FF	81	Yes
Vulture	Heavy	Clan	60	Reactive	85	No
Loki	Heavy	Clan	65	FF	83	No
Nova Cat	Heavy	Clan	70	Laser Ref.	73	No
Thor	Heavy	Clan	70	FF	85	Yes

CONTINUED ON PAGE 54

CONTINUED FROM PAGE 53

'Mech	Class	Chassis Tech Type	Max Tonnage	Armor Type	Top Speed (KpH)	Jump Jets
Mad Cat	Heavy	Clan	75	FF	85	No
Awesome	Assault	IS	80	FF	75	No
Mauler	Assault	IS	90	Reactive	65	No
Atlas	Assault	IS	100	FF	57	No
Mad Cat MK. II	Assault	Clan	90	FF	73	Yes
Daishi	Assault	Clan	100	FF	51	No

Table 3.23 breaks down the number of armor and internal structure Hit Points for each 'Mech by body part. The data is displayed in the following format: maximum armor/front armor/rear armor/internal structure.

Table 3.23: Armor and Internal Structure Hit Points by Body Part

'Mech	Head	Arms (Each)	Right/Left Torso	Center Torso	Legs (Each)
Osiris	9/9/–/3	12/12/–/6	18/15/–/9	42/27/12/21	30/24/–/18
Raven	9/9/–/3	18/18/–/9	24/21/–/12	48/30/12/24	42/33/–/21
Cougar	9/9/–/3	18/15/–/9	24/15/–/12	48/21/9/24	42/18/–/21
Chimera	9/8/–/3	18/16/–/9	30/20/–/15	54/24/12/27	48/32/–/24
Hellspawn	9/9/–/3	24/24/–/12	30/27/–/15	60/36/15/30	54/39/–/27
Uziel	9/9/–/3	30/27/–/15	36/30/–/18	66/45/18/33	60/27/–/30
Bushwacker	9/9/–/3	30/24/–/15	42/36/–/21	72/51/15/36	66/30/–/33
Shadow Cat	9/9/–/3	24/24/–/12	30/30/–/15	60/42/15/30	54/48/–/27
Argus	18/18/–/6	36/24/–/18	48/30/–/24	78/40/18/39	66/28/–/33
Catapult	18/18/–/6	36/30/–/18	48/28/–/24	84/44/12/42	72/30/–/36
Thanatos	18/18/–/6	42/39/–/21	54/51/–/27	90/57/27/45	78/54/–/39
Vulture	18/18/–/6	36/18/–/18	48/24/–/24	78/32/10/39	66/28/–/33
Loki	18/18/–/6	36/24/–/18	48/30/–/24	84/51/24/42	72/42/–/36
Nova Cat	18/18/–/6	42/34/–/21	54/32/–/27	90/38/20/45	72/36/–/36
Thor	18/18/–/6	42/33/–/21	54/36/–/27	90/57/18/45	72/42/–/36
Mad Cat	18/18/–/6	42/33/–/21	54/42/–/27	90/60/27/45	78/45/–/39
Awesome	27/27/–/9	48/42/–/24	60/57/–/30	96/66/27/48	84/66/–/42
Mauler	27/22/–/9	54/24/–/27	66/32/–/33	102/54/16/51	90/28/–/45

'Mech	Head	Arms (Each)	Right/Left Torso	Center Torso	Legs (Each)
Atlas	27/27/–/9	66/54/–/33	72/69/–/36	108/78/33/54	96/78/–/48
Mad Cat MK. II	27/27/–/9	54/39/–/27	66/48/–/33	102/69/27/51	90/54/–/45
Daishi	27/27/–/9	66/42/–/33	72/57/–/36	108/72/24/54	96/57/–/48

The Tonnage Breakdown chart (Table 3.24) displays the raw tonnage of each 'Mech's default configuration in its component parts.

Table 3.24: Tonnage Breakdown

'Mech	Internal Structure	Engine	Cockpit	Jump Jets	Armor	Heat Sinks	Weapons/ Components
Osiris	1.5	7.5	3	2	5	0	11
Raven	3.5	4.5	3	N/A	6.5	0	17.5
Cougar	1.5	5.5	3	2	4.5	1	17.5
Chimera	2	7	3	3	9	0	16
Hellspawn	2	10	3	3	8	0	19
Uziel	2.5	7.5	3	3	8	4	22
Bushwacker	5.5	10	3	N/A	8.5	0	28
Shadow Cat	2	8.5	3	3	9	1	18.5
Argus	3.5	9.5	3	N/A	12	0	32
Catapult	3	10.5	3	4	12.5	1	31
Thanatos	4	17	3	4	13	0	34
Vulture	6	12	3	N/A	10	1	28
Loki	6.5	9.5	3	N/A	9.5	1	35.5
Nova Cat	4	9.5	3	N/A	14	14	25.5
Thor	7	14	3	4	10.5	1	30.5
Mad Cat	3.5	20	3	N/A	11.5	5	32
Awesome	8	15	3	N/A	15	10	29
Mauler	9	17	3	N/A	13	0	48
Atlas	10	18	3	N/A	18	3	48
Mad Cat MK. II	4.5	26	3	6	13.5	0	37
Daishi	10	15	3	N/A	14.5	10	47.5

Building a Better 'Mech

The MechLab (see Figure 3.1) represents the ultimate level of control in the game. It allows you to customize your BattleMech in just about any way you can imagine.

In the MechLab, you can change the following aspects of your 'Mech:

- ▣▶ **Engine Rating:** The size of the 'Mech's engine.

- ▣▶ **Armor:** The type, total weight, and placement of your Battle-Mech's armor protection.

- ▣▶ **Heat Sinks:** The number and placement of additional heat sinks the 'Mech carries.

- ▣▶ **Jump Jets:** You can add Jump Jets to the design of any 'Mech that can use them.

- ▣▶ **Electronics:** Add advanced electronics to any 'Mech that can support them. Feel free to remove them as well.

- ▣▶ **Weapons and Ammo:** The number and placement of the 'Mech's weapon systems, and the amount of ammunition carried by those weapons requiring it.

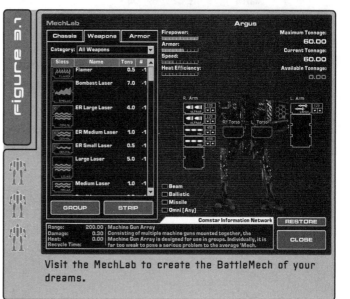

TIP

Every 'Mech has to have an engine, so the MechLab won't let you build a 'Mech without one. If you strip a 'Mech of all its equipment, it is automatically equipped with the smallest engine available.

figure 3.1

Visit the MechLab to create the BattleMech of your dreams.

In the campaign game, what you can and can't add to your 'Mech is determined by the equipment you have on hand at the start of any given mission. Additional war materiel and 'Mech chassis are added to your inventory in the form of salvage recovered after successful battles. Further items can be obtained through shadier means by trading your on-hand stock for black market equipment (see the game manual for further details).

'Mech design is a personal affair, and as such we won't presume to lay down any hard and fast rules regarding the process. We will, however, give you some basic tips to keep in mind to avoid creating a 'Mech that will be DOA on the battlefield:

- **Determine your 'Mech's primary role.** This is the most important aspect of 'Mech design. The 'Mechs that work best are designed primarily for a single task—long-range combat, speed, prolonged survivability, and so on. By trying to build a 'Mech of all trades, you'll generally end up with a 'Mech that has no concrete strengths.

- **Choose a loadout appropriate to your 'Mech's chassis.** A 35-ton BattleMech can't carry the same amount of weapons and armor that a 100-ton 'Mech can. At the same time, don't expect a 100-ton assault 'Mech to move like a 35-ton light 'Mech no matter *what* size engine it has.

- **Add long-range weapons only if you need them.** Long-range strike capability is a nice option, especially if you know you'll be up against 'Mechs that can shred you at close range. If you don't know what you'll be up against, adding one long-range weapon (preferably a missile rack) is a good compromise. Eliminate long-range weapons altogether if you're building a 'Mech for close-range battles.

NOTE

To get an idea of the types of weapons, armor, and equipment appropriate to each 'Mech size and type, check out the default designs described earlier in this chapter.

- **Short-range weapons are for weenies.** That's a bit harsh, but short-range weapons require that you be pretty much right on top of a target in order to use them. They're fine for close brawls, but they're useless against an enemy who keeps his distance. In short, despite the fact that they're small and light, their disadvantages tend to outweigh their advantages.

Medium-range weapons are the keys to success. Medium-range weapons are the perfect compromise between size and versatility. They give you more striking power on a per-weapon basis than their short-range counterparts, while allowing you to keep your distance from the enemy. Unless you're building a 'Mech for some specific combat purpose, you're best served with an arsenal composed primarily of medium-range weapons.

Beams are best—usually. Beam weapons have three major advantages as a group over ballistic weapons and missiles: they're lighter, easier to hit with, and they never run out of ammunition. You could do worse than an all-beam 'Mech—as long as you account for the extra heat that these weapons produce with lots of heat sinks.

> 'Mech design is a tricky business, and not one that should be attempted until you learn the nuances of 'Mech and weapon performance. The best way to do so is by playing the game for a while using default configurations.

If you can't stand the heat...add a few heat sinks. Every engine comes with its own set of 10 heat sinks. In smaller 'Mech designs, this is usually sufficient. In larger 'Mechs, however, the sheer number of weapons carried can create more heat than the engine can handle. Instead of using up all your available space and weight on weapons, save yourself some future headaches and throw in a couple of extra heat sinks.

Non-'Mech Vehicles

Much of the combat in *MechWarrior 4* pits your 'Mech against enemy 'Mechs. These encounters are, by far, the most challenging combat engagements in the game—but they're not the only ones. Throughout the single-player campaign, you also encounter a wide array of land, sea, and air vehicles that must be dealt with. While none of these is any match for a BattleMech individually, they can still be a nuisance—especially when attacking en masse. It pays to know what you're up against when you encounter these vehicles.

Table 3.25 lists all of the non-'Mech vehicles in the game and their vital statistics. For the lowdown on the armaments they carry, see the weapon descriptions in Chapter 4: Weapons and Components.

Table 3.25: Statistics of Non-'Mech Vehicles

Vehicle	Max Speed (KpH)	Weapons
APC	75.6	–
Bulldog	64.8	SRM2 (2), Large Laser, Machine Gun
Condor	86.4	Medium Laser (2), AC5, Machine Gun
Destroyer	–	Long Tom (4), LRM20 (2)
Harasser	97.2	SRM4 (3)
Hrothgar	–	PPC (4), Gauss Rifle (4), Large Laser (4)
LRM Carrier	54	LRM10 (3)
Nightshade	126	STRK2 (2)
Patrol Boat 1	–	Ultra AC5
Patrol Boat 2	–	Large Laser
Peregrine	126	STRK2 (2)
Shilone	198	Bombs
SRM Carrier	54	SRM6 (3)
Talon	–	Large Laser (4), ER Large Laser (4), LRM10 (3)
Vedette	82.8	Ultra AC5, Machine Gun

weapons and components

Now that you know the operational strengths and weaknesses of every 'Mech design, it's time to look at what gives these behemoths their teeth. In this chapter, we'll detail all the weapon systems and components that your 'Mech can carry and discuss strategies for their use in battle.

'Mechs are the most sophisticated and deadly war machines ever created. So, is it any wonder that there is a vast arsenal of deadly devices with which they can be equipped? Weapons in MechWarrior 4 fall into three basic categories: beam/energy weapons, ballistic weapons, and missiles.

Unless otherwise noted, there are both Inner Sphere and Clan versions of every weapon. The two versions function almost identically, but Clan weapons almost always have better range and can inflict more damage than their Inner Sphere counterparts. Other differences are noted below on a case-by-case basis.

Beam/Energy Weapons

This category of weapons includes anything that uses raw energy—rather than physical ammunition—to inflict damage. This characteristic is one of the major advantages of this weapon type. Beam/energy devices never require extra space and weight for ammunition, nor will they ever run out of ammo on the battlefield.

On the downside, beam weapons generally don't pack as much punch per shot as their projectile-firing cousins. Another problem is heat. Beam weapons run a lot hotter than ballistic weapons per shot (again, on average) and can overheat if fired too quickly. Needless to say, this can lead to some serious problems on the battlefield.

MechWarrior 4 includes 17 different beam/energy weapons (see Figure 4.1), all of which fall into 5 categories: Beam Lasers, Pulse Lasers, Bombast Lasers, Particle Projection Cannons (PPCs), and Flamers.

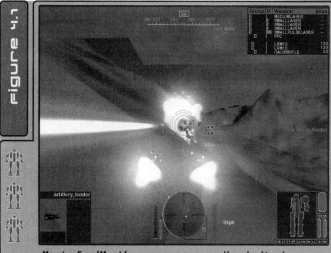

Figure 4.1

Most of a 'Mech's awesome power lies in its devastating arsenal of weapons.

Beam Lasers

Beam Lasers are the most basic form of beam/energy weapon. When you pull the trigger, they fire a continuous beam that inflicts damage for the duration of the shot. Once a Beam Laser hits its target, the beam "sticks" there for the duration of the shot.

Beam Lasers come in three sizes: small, medium, and large. The larger the laser, the greater its range and power. Clan lasers produce more heat and weigh more than their Inner Sphere counterparts.

TIP

Generally speaking, Small Lasers aren't very effective weapons. They're only useful at short ranges, and they aren't powerful enough to inflict significant damage on their own. Unless you're able to group several Small Lasers to fire in tandem, use the space and weight for something else.

Pulse Lasers

Pulse Lasers are laser machine guns. They operate in pretty much the same manner as Beam Lasers, although they fire much shorter beams and have shorter recycle times (see Figure 4.2). As with Beam Lasers, there are three sizes: small, medium, and large.

These weapons have both advantages and disadvantages when compared to Beam Lasers. On the plus side, they have the potential to inflict more damage than their beam counterparts. For example, 10 seconds' worth of damage from a Large

Pulse Laser inflicts 20.96 points of damage, whereas a standard Large Laser inflicts only 15.

Of course, that's assuming that all the pulses hit. The downside to Pulse Lasers is that each pulse is a separate beam, and as such there's no guarantee that every burst will find its mark. Every pulse is a tenth of a second in duration, and it takes as long as 1.25 seconds to recycle between pulses. So more than 10 real-time seconds are required to deliver 10 seconds' worth of damage with a pulse laser.

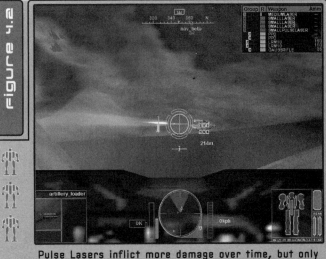

Pulse Lasers inflict more damage over time, but only if you can keep the target in your sights.

Bombast Lasers

The Bombast Laser (note that there is no Clan version of the Bombast Laser) is the most powerful laser in the game. You're in control of how much damage it inflicts. Every time you pull the trigger, the weapon begins to charge. When it reaches maximum strength, it fires automatically at full power. You can, of course, release the trigger at any time during the charging interval to fire off a less powerful blast.

Despite the fact that Pulse Lasers produce less heat per shot than Beam Lasers, excessive warmth can build up quickly during a prolonged conflict. Don't let the low heat numbers for these weapons lull you into firing them constantly.

At full power, the Bombast Laser edges out every other laser in the game in terms of damage. It also takes up the same amount of space as a Large Beam or Pulse Laser, and has a shorter recycle time than any Beam Laser.

Of course, there's always a catch. Actually, in this case, there are two. First is the power-up time for firing a full-strength shot. In order to deliver maximum damage, you need to keep your target lined up until the weapon fires. That can be very difficult unless you're quite skilled or your target isn't moving. The other problem associated with this weapon is the heat it produces. At 8 points per shot, it is tied with the Clan ER Large Laser as the hottest laser in the game. And when you take the Bombast Laser's shorter recycle time into account, this weapon builds heat up faster than any other laser.

Bottom line: avoid using this weapon until you're practiced in both marksmanship and heat management.

Particle Projection Cannons (PPCs)

Particle Projection Cannons (PPCs) do as much as the Bombast Lasers in the damage department. The Clan version of this device can actually reach out and "touch" someone as far as 900 meters away!

PPCs are similar to Gauss Rifles (see the entry below on Gauss Rifles) in range and damage, but have the advantage of never running out of ammunition. Unfortunately, their disadvantages outweigh this one positive, especially if you lack experience with using them.

NOTE

PPCs are the only beam weapons that have a travel time—that is, they do not hit instantaneously like other beams. In this respect, they behave like ballistic weapons.

The main problem is heat. A 'Mech bristling with PPCs is a fearsome thing for your enemies to behold, but after a few quick shots—especially if you're firing linked PPCs—the heat will go off the scale. You have to plan for heat problems when you're using PPCs. When outfitting a BattleMech that uses these weapons, make sure that you have plenty of heat sinks on hand. Even then, keep an eye on your heat gauge in any prolonged confrontation.

TIP

When hit by a PPC, your HUD goes to static for a few seconds due to the massive interference caused by this weapon. This effect is greatly reduced if your 'Mech is equipped with Guardian ECM.

Flamers

Flamers are unique in that they're not supposed to inflict a great deal of damage. Instead of bashing the enemy, they push your opponent toward an overheat state.

Unlike the other Clan beam weapons, Clan Flamers neither inflict increased damage nor have longer range. They are, however, lighter than their Inner Sphere counterparts.

While Flamers are a fun way to fight opposing 'Mechs, they have serious disadvantages. Their short firing range is a detriment, as is the way that they generate a lot of heat for *you* as well as your opponent. Flamers produce more heat on average than most other beam/energy weapons (Bombast Lasers, Large Lasers, and PPCs aside).

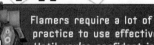

TIP

Flamers require a lot of practice to use effectively. Until you're confident in your skills, you're better off filling the two weapon slots taken up by a Flamer with something more practical, like a Medium Laser.

NOTE

Throughout this book and in the game itself, weapons are referred to as short-, medium-, or long-range weapons. In terms of actual distance, this breaks down as follows: short range (0–299 meters), medium range (300–599 meters), and long range (>600 meters).

Beam/Energy Weapon Statistics

Table 4.1 lists the vital statistics for all of *MechWarrior 4*'s beam/energy weapons. The following statistics are listed for each:

- **Range:** The range of the weapon in meters.

- **Recycle:** The amount of time after a shot before the weapon can be fired again (in seconds).

- **Heat:** The number of heat points produced each time the weapon is fired.

- **Damage:** The amount of damage the specified weapon inflicts on a target per hit.

⬤ **Weight:** The weight of the weapon (in tons).

⬤ **Space:** The amount of space the weapon takes up in a 'Mech (measured in the number of slots it fills).

Table 4.1: Beam/Energy Weapon Statistics

Weapon	Range	Recycle	Heat	Damage	Weight	Space
Small Laser	150	1	0.1	0.3	0.5	1
Medium Laser	300	3	0.6	1.2	1	1
Large Laser	600	5	5	7.5	5	2
Clan ER Small Laser	200	1	0.2	0.35	0.5	1
Clan ER Medium Laser	400	3	1.2	1.5	1	1
Clan ER Large Laser	800	5	8	8	4	2
Small Pulse Laser	150	0.25	0.05	0.15	1	1
Medium Pulse Laser	300	0.75	0.3	0.6	2	1
Large Pulse Laser	600	1.25	1.75	2.62	7	2
Clan ER Small Pulse Laser	200	0.25	0.12	0.27	1.5	1
Clan ER Medium Pulse Laser	400	0.75	0.6	0.75	2	1
Clan ER Large Pulse Laser	800	1.25	3	3	6	2
Bombast Laser	500	4	8	10*	7	2
PPC	750	6	10	10	7	3
Clan ER PPC	900	8	15	14	6	3
Flamer	150	4	4	1	1	2
Clan Flamer	150	4	4	1	0.5	2

* Damage for maximum charge.

Ballistic Weapons

This category covers all projectile weapons in the game that do *not* fire missiles. This includes a wide variety of cannons, from small machine gun arrays to heavy artillery.

On average, ballistic weapons deliver more damage per shot than beam weapons of similar size and weight. They also generate less heat when fired. These two factors alone make them extremely valuable offensively.

They have two major drawbacks, however. Unlike beam weapons, ballistic weapons rely on ammunition. That means that they will eventually become useless in a prolonged firefight. The need for ammunition also figures into their second disadvantage, which is weight. Not only are the weapons themselves heavier than comparable beam weapons, their ammunition load significantly adds to your 'Mech's weight. That means a trade-off between 'Mech performance/speed and weapons loadout.

Ballistic weapons fall into four basic categories: Machine Gun Arrays, Autocannons, Gauss Rifles, and Long Tom Cannons.

Machine Gun Arrays

Machine Gun Arrays are the least powerful ballistic weapons available (see Figure 4.3). They consist of a group of machine guns mounted in a cluster (a single machine gun would have little effect on something as tough as a BattleMech!), all of which fire simultaneously.

Machine Gun Arrays aren't very powerful and can only be used at short range.

As one might expect, even when mounted in clusters, machine guns have only minimal effect against the thick armor found on most BattleMechs. These weapons are only useful against small 'Mechs and non-'Mech vehicles.

Autocannons

Autocannons come in several different varieties, each with unique characteristics and performance specifications.

Basic Autocannons

Basic Autocannons are giant machine guns. They fire large-caliber ammunition in bursts, inflicting a decent amount of damage. There are two varieties of the basic Autocannon: the AC5 and the AC10. Both are Inner Sphere weapons (there are no Clan versions). The AC5 has 50% greater range, a much faster rate of fire, and carries more ammunition than the AC10, but at the expense of inflicting significantly less damage.

Unlike Machine Gun Arrays, Autocannons can inflict enough damage to be useful against heavy targets.

Ultra Autocannons

Ultra Autocannons are to basic Autocannons what Pulse Lasers are to Beam Lasers. They fire dual bursts of ammo separated by short intervals, greatly increasing the long-term damage potential. Two varieties are available: the AC2 and the AC5. As with the basic Autocannons, the larger of the two is slower and is limited to shorter range, but inflicts more damage. Unlike most other weapons, the Clan Ultra Autocannons are nearly identical to their Inner Sphere counterparts (except for their lighter weight).

There are trade-offs between these weapons and the basic versions. Ultra Autocannons do twice as much damage as the basic variety since they fire twice as many shots when you pull the trigger. The negative aspects are that it's harder to hit with both shots due to the delay and that they chew through ammo at twice the rate.

LBX Scattershots

The third variety of Autocannon is stylistically different than the other two. Instead of firing a stream of bullets like a machine gun, it fires a group of slugs in shotgun fashion. The end result is a slower Autocannon that packs a lot more

NOTE

LBX Scattershots exhibit a damage drop-off over distance because of the slug spread. Per-shot damage is decreased by 50% beyond half of the weapon's maximum range.

shot per punch. There are two varieties: the LBX-AC10 and the LBX-AC20. The larger of the two has less range but much more power. As with Ultra Autocannons, the Clan versions of this weapon are identical to the Inner Sphere version except for their lighter weight.

Even though this is the slowest type of Autocannon, two features make it worthwhile. First, it is an extremely powerful weapon. That power comes at the expense of higher heat and slower recycle time than most ballistic weapons, but it's an acceptable trade-off. Second, the spread pattern of the shot makes it possible to strike more than one body part on a target 'Mech. Most other weapons hit only one body part at a time.

Gauss Rifles

Gauss Rifles are among the most fearsome ballistic weapons available. They propel a 41.66-kilogram slug over incredible ranges, delivering huge amounts of damage (see Figure 4.4). Gauss Rifles come in light and heavy varieties. The Clan version of the standard Gauss Rifle differs from the Inner Sphere variety only in its lighter weight (there is no light Clan version of this weapon).

Figure 4.4

The powerful Gauss Rifle is one of the finest weapons available.

The price you pay for such awesome firepower is space and weight. These factors make Gauss Rifles impractical for smaller 'Mechs. Another major drawback is the weapon's long recycle time. With six to eight seconds between shots, you definitely need some backup weapons to supplement your armament.

Long Tom Cannons

Long Tom Cannons are direct-fire artillery pieces that are extremely deadly in the right hands. The Clan doesn't have a version of this weapon.

This is the most powerful ballistic weapon in the game, but its power doesn't come without cost. Most problematic is the lack of an automatic targeting system;

you have to tilt your 'Mech's torso back and forth to set the weapon's range. The shell is then fired in an arc in the direction you're facing when you pull the trigger.

While the Long Tom produces *very* satisfying results when used properly, the learning curve for employing it properly is so steep that it makes the weapon impractical in most circumstances. A Gauss Rifle is generally more useful, and by employing it instead of a Long Tom, you'll save four tons of weight to boot.

Ballistic Weapon Statistics

Table 4.2 lists the stats of the ballistic weapons. The statistics shown are the same as those in Table 4.1 with the following additions:

Ammo: The maximum number of ammo rounds for the weapon.

Ammo/Ton: The number of rounds of ammo per one ton of weight.

Table 4.2: Ballistic Weapon Statistics

Weapon	Range	Recycle	Heat	Damage	Weight	Slots	Ammo	Ammo/Ton
Machine Gun Array	150	0.3	0	0.2	2	1	1350	450
Clan Machine Gun Array	200	0.3	0	0.3	2	1	1800	600
AC5	600	1.5	0.2	2	8	1	350	120
AC10	400	4	0.6	9	13	2	216	36
Ultra AC2	900	1	0.1	1	8	1	720	240
Ultra AC5	600	1.5	0.15	2	10	1	360	120
Clan Ultra AC2	900	1	0.1	1	6	1	720	240
Clan Ultra AC5	600	1.5	0.15	2	8	1	360	120
LBX-AC10	450	4	1	14	12	2	216	36
LBX-AC20	300	6	2	24	15	3	180	20
Clan LBX-AC10	450	4	1	14	10	2	216	36
Clan LBX-AC20	300	6	2	24	12	3	180	20

CONTINUED ON PAGE 70

CONTINUED FROM PAGE 69

Weapon	Range	Recycle	Heat	Damage	Weight	Slots	Ammo	Ammo/Ton
Light Gauss Rifle	1200	6	0.8	12	13	2	180	30
Gauss Rifle	800	8	1	17	16	3	216	24
Clan Gauss Rifle	800	8	1	17	13	3	216	24
Long Tom Cannon	700	7	14	25	20	3	162	18

Missiles

Missiles represent something of a compromise between ballistic and beam weapons. Like ballistic devices, missile racks have limited ammunition. They do, however, tend to be lighter than ballistic weapons of comparable damage value. And while missiles produce more heat on average than their ballistic counterparts, they generally run cooler than beam weapons. Most missiles fire in clusters and, therefore, have the potential to strike multiple 'Mech body parts in a single salvo.

Aside from these factors, there are two considerations that are unique to missiles. First, consider that most of them lock onto targets. While this adds a bit of time to the aiming process, it does ensure greater accuracy. On the downside, some warheads can be shot down by antimissile systems before they reach their target.

There are four basic missile types: Short-Range, Medium-Range, Long-Range, and Thunderbolt.

Short-Range Missiles (SRMs and STRKs)

In terms of short-range weaponry, nothing gives you more bang for the buck than Short-Range Missiles. Their damage is significantly higher than any other weapon in this range group. There are two different types of Short-Range Missiles:

SRM: SRMs are used by the Inner Sphere. These missiles don't lock on. Instead, they are high-speed direct-fire missiles that fly in the direction that the 'Mech is pointed in when fired. They come in three different varieties: SRM2, SRM4, and SRM6. Their main advantage over STRKs is that they aren't affected by antimissile systems. The disadvantage is that they are much less accurate.

STRK: STRKs are Clan weapons. Unlike SRMs, these missiles lock onto their targets. With terrain-following capability and the ability to turn on a dime, these weapons are far more dangerous than SRMs. STRK missiles inflict more damage than SRMs as well. The only downside is that they generate more heat and can be stopped by antimissile defenses. There are three varieties: STRK2, STRK4, and STRK6.

Medium-Range Missiles (MRMs)

> **TIP**
>
> Unless you need long-range striking power, MRMs are the best missiles available. Despite the extra weight and space, they are acceptable substitutes for SRMs in all but the smallest 'Mechs.

As one would assume, MRMs have greater range and can inflict more damage than Short-Range Missiles. They are also considerably heavier and have a longer recycle time.

MRMs have a cascade firing effect. Holding down the trigger launches swarm after swarm of 10 deadly missiles at quarter-second intervals. There are four types of MRM racks: 10, 20, 30, and 40. These numbers indicate the number of missiles that are ready for each recycling of the weapon. For example, an MRM40 can fire four 10-missile clusters before it has to recycle.

Long-Range Missiles (LRMs)

Long-Range Missiles (LRMs) are the mainstays of long-range combat. They are the most effective weapons available in terms of heat and rate of fire for combat over significant distances (see Figure 4.5). There are four types of LRM

Figure 4.5

Use Long-Range Missiles to soften up your targets before you move in for the kill.

racks: 5, 10, 15, and 20. The Clan versions of these missiles are identical to their Inner Sphere counterparts except for weight—which in this case is nearly 50% less! These missiles require a lock in order to be launched.

The only reason to use LRMs is if you need long-range striking power. You're much better served by the more powerful MRMs in medium- and short-range encounters.

> TIP
>
> Once you obtain a lock on a target, you can shoot over obstacles by tilting your 'Mech back and firing the missile in an arc. Remember that while all missiles track their targets in the open, only STRKs avoid terrain obstacles on their own.

Thunderbolt Missiles

Unlike all other missile racks in the game, the Thunderbolt fires a single missile instead of a cluster. Like SRMs, this is a dumb-fire missile (meaning that it requires no lock and doesn't track its target).

Thunderbolt Missiles fall into the same category as Flamers and Long Tom Cannons. They are very specialized and require a lot of skill (or luck) to use effectively. On top of this, Thunderbolts are slow (hence easy to avoid), heavy, and space-intensive. The one advantage this missile has over all others is in its huge punch. When it hits, the target 'Mech gets seriously knocked around, making targeting difficult until the shaking stops. Still, the real damage inflicted is less than that of an average missile. It's up to you to decide whether the impact effects make investing in a Thunderbolt a worthwhile option.

Missile Statistics

Table 4.3 lists the statistics for all missile types.

Table 4.3: missile statistics

Weapon	Range	Recycle	Heat	Damage	Weight	Slots	Ammo	Ammo/Ton
SRM2	250	2	0.4	2	2	1	360	120
SRM4	250	2	0.6	4	3	1	360	120
SRM6	250	2	0.8	6	4	2	720	120

Weapon	Range	Recycle	Heat	Damage	Weight	Slots	Ammo	Ammo/Ton
STRK2	250	3	0.6	2.4	2	1	360	120
STRK4	250	3	0.9	4.8	3	1	360	120
STRK6	250	3	1.2	7.2	4	2	720	120
MRM10	400	5	2.4	8	5	1	720	240
MRM20	400	4	4.8	16	8	2	1440	240
MRM30	400	5	6	24	11	2	1440	240
MRM40	400	5	7.2	32	13	3	2160	240
LRM5	1000	6	1.2	4	3	1	720	240
LRM10	1000	6	2.4	8	6	1	720	240
LRM15	1000	6	3	12	8	2	1440	240
LRM20	1000	6	3.6	16	11	2	1440	240
Clan LRM5	1000	6	1.2	4	2	1	720	240
Clan LRM10	1000	6	2.4	8	3.5	1	720	240
Clan LRM15	1000	6	3	12	4.5	2	1440	240
Clan LRM20	1000	6	3.6	16	6	2	1440	240
Thunderbolt	1000	8	7	23	14	3	135	15

Additional Features and Components

The rest of this chapter looks at the additional weapons and components available for your 'Mech. While most of these items are not offensive weaponry, all of them can enhance your 'Mech's combat performance and/or survivability.

AMS/LAMS: An antimissile system is a great way to minimize damage if you're up against missile-toting enemies. Just remember that these systems can't block SRMs or MRMs. The AMS is Inner Sphere, the LAMS Clan.

NARC Beacon: When you're part of a force with lots of long-range missile capability, sacrificing a little weapon space on one of the 'Mechs for a NARC Beacon is a good move to ensure accurate missile barrages. Just remember that units equipped with an ECM system cause NARCs to fail more quickly than normal. NARC Beacons have a range of 450 meters (600 for the Clan version).

Beagle Active Probe: This is a great enhancement that increases your active sensor range. It's an excellent aid, but it also decreases the amount of time it takes for your opponents to lock missiles on you by 30%!

Guardian ECM: A perfect system to employ if you need to sneak up on an enemy 'Mech or installation without being detected. Unfortunately, like the Beagle Active Probe, it decreases the amount of time it takes the enemy to achieve a missile lock on you.

Light Amplification: This night vision package is safer than turning on your searchlight. If you're going on a night mission and you have an extra ton of weight to spare (and your 'Mech design allows it), this item is highly recommended.

Flare Launcher: Fires flares to a distance of 360 meters. Flares are decent as a light source, but they're even better for blinding enemy 'Mechs equipped with Light Amplification systems.

Artillery: In some missions, you have the opportunity to call in a friendly artillery strike. If you see "Artillery" in your HUD weapon listing, use it! Any additional firepower you can get will always be helpful.

High Explosives: This weapon option is only available in multi-player, and then only on the Cougar, Raven, and Osiris 'Mechs. It allows you to attach packs of high explosives to your 'Mech when you're equipping it. If triggered in combat, it causes your 'Mech to self-destruct. Everything within a 25-meter radius takes significant damage for each pack of high explosives you attach. Try it...it's fun!

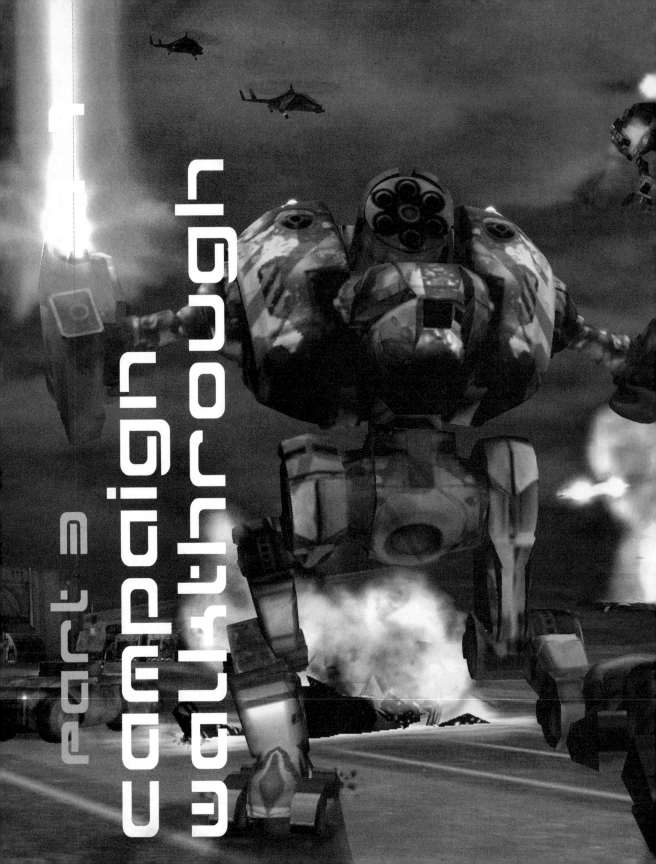

Part 3

campaign
walkthrough

*P*art 3: Campaign Walkthrough covers all of the solo missions in MechWarrior 4: Vengeance. Every walkthrough contains the mission briefing, recommended 'Mech and weapon loadouts, and tactics for successfully completing each objective.

Chapter 5 covers the first operation, "Optimism," which includes the game's initial four lunar-based missions. In Chapter 6, you'll find complete walkthroughs for the four arctic excursions that make up the second operation, "Early Success." Chapter 7 features walkthroughs for the three alpine missions that make up "First Command," the third operation. Strategies for the six desert missions of the fourth operation, "Building Forces," are presented in Chapter 8. Chapter 9 offers walkthroughs for the three swamp-based missions in the fifth operation, "The Greater Good." Inside Chapter 10 you'll find detailed tips for fighting through the five urban missions comprising Operation 6, "The Darkest Hour." Chapter 11 contains the walkthrough for the final mission of the seventh and last operation, "Final Victory."

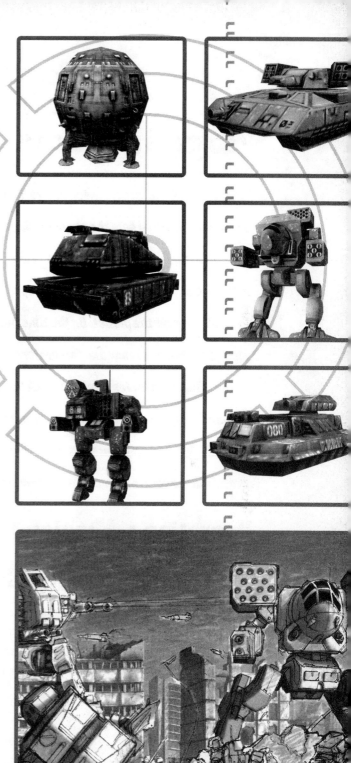

operation 1: "optimism" missions

Set on the cold Kentares IV moon where 'Mech heat management is not critical, the first

campaign operation sets the stage for the subsequent, more dangerous missions.

During "Optimism" you will operate in a support role and won't direct other

BattleMechs. The goal is to greatly hamper Steiner's ability to easily deploy

BattleMechs over the planet. By the time the mission ends, you will hopefully also have

wiped out Steiner's lunar and far-orbit reconnaissance capabilities.

This chapter includes complete walkthroughs for the four missions that comprise the

"Optimism" operation. Though you are participating in live combat, enemy 'Mechs aren't

particularly tough and you should use these missions to further familiarize yourself

with the game controls, 'Mech and weapon selection, and combat maneuvers.

Operation 1, Mission 1: Destroy Communications Relay

Mission Briefing: Destroy lunar communications relay. Our rebellion starts here. We are going to raid and destroy the key component of the Steiner communications net. Enemy forces are light and resistance should be minimal. Destroy the three communications relay stations, and Steiner's communications will be cut off from Kentares IV.

MechLab

Since this is the game's first mission, you aren't offered any selection of 'Mechs to choose from. Select the Shadow Cat from the 'Mech menu. If you wish, head to the MechLab and customize its armor layout.

You're facing weak enemies in this first encounter—APCs, Bulldog tanks, Short-Range Missiles (SRMs), and turrets present the greatest danger. With the MechLab, you could modify the Shadow Cat's armor positioning and place more armor near the front. If you do, attempt to keep all hostile targets in sight. Your armor will be weaker from the rear, so avoid turning your back or side to an enemy vehicle or stationary foe.

Battle Plan

Objective: Destroy all three communications towers.

You begin the mission within a cutscene where you watch you and your two lance-mates (not under your control) launched from the dropship to the moon surface below. As you descend, command elaborates on your mission objective. Ahead of your current position lies the main communications station. Expect light defenses as you approach. You're then shown the communications relay stations. According to command, these structures are more durable and will require heavier weaponry to destroy.

As soon as you gain control of your 'Mech, your two lancemates will start toward the primary objective ahead. Increase your 'Mech's speed to full. Follow the road into the crater that contains the listening post and communications buildings. There's only one navigation point available in this mission. Locate your NAV point in your directional finder. Alternatively, you can simply follow your lancemates and be led to the primary objective target (see Figure 5.1).

Your lancemates will have already begun annihilating enemy targets before you enter the crater. Join them by targeting the nearest enemy vehicle or turret. You'll encounter many foes inside the small communications base, though none should provide much resistance. Bulldog tanks and Long-Range Missile (LRM) emplacements (which surround the crater) will offer the most trouble. Target them, then approach and blast away with lasers or missiles.

As you move through the camp, try to avoid smashing into buildings or stationary vehicles—it's practically the only way you can suffer moderate amounts of damage here. Use this relatively basic mission for additional training. Practice cycling through enemy targets, grouping and using your available weapons, and so on. This mission's targets are smaller than the enemy 'Mechs you'll face later on, so take the time to work on your hit-to-miss efficiency.

Follow your lancemates into the crater containing the listening post and light vehicle guard.

During your rampage through the communications base, several enemy transports will begin retreating. Command alerts you to the developing situation and orders you to intercept the moving transports and prevent them from escaping the area.

Mid-Mission Objective: Destroy escaping enemy units.

Since this first operation takes place on the Kentares IV moon, you don't need to be overly concerned with heat management. Feel free to unleash your weaponry at will. If you're given a heat warning, lay off the weapons momentarily.

Several transports begin fleeing the crater communications base. These transports immediately head toward the exit roads that lie opposite from the road where you and your lancemates entered. As soon as you're ordered to neutralize the mobile units, cycle through available enemy targets until you locate the nearest enemy labeled "transport." More than one escaping enemy unit must be taken care of, so remember to work quickly. Lock onto the nearest transport and increase your 'Mech's speed to full.

Fire your weapons at the transport as you approach. If you fail to destroy the transport on the first pass, consider smashing your 'Mech into it. This will destroy the fleeing vehicle. You may take minor damage, but ramming the transport will save you the time and bother of circling around for another pass. Alternatively, follow close behind the transport and decelerate your 'Mech. Once you're slowed down, it becomes extremely easy to line up your crosshairs and annihilate the vehicle with your weaponry.

WARNING

There are multiple transports, so don't grow complacent after annihilating the first fleeing vehicle. Quickly cycle through the enemy targets until you locate another transport escaping the communications base. If you slowed down your 'Mech for the first assault, return to full speed now and attack the remaining transports.

Once the fleeing transports are destroyed, begin your assault on the communications towers and listening post. Cycle through enemy targets until you've locked onto one of these buildings. There are three communications towers to destroy in addition to the lone listening post, which resides between the triangle formed by the three communications stations.

Approach the stations and listening post closely and fire off your weapons. Destroy the three communications stations, and the listening post in between will explode in a huge ball of shredded metal and flame (see Figure 5.2). The mission ends in success once its primary objective has been completed.

Figure 5.2

The durable communications towers and listening post require some heavy pounding with your weaponry.

Operation I, Mission I serves mainly as a shooting gallery. Enemy targets are plentiful, but don't offer much resistance. Because the mission is so straightforward, there's no real change to the walkthrough outlined in this section. If you wish, concentrate more on objective targets (the transports, the communications relay stations, and the listening post) while your lancemates annihilate the tanks, APCs, and LRM emplacements around the base. Instead of running through the base and destroying the mostly harmless enemy targets, position yourself near the roads leading away from the communications station (opposite from your entrance road) and await the objective to neutralize the runaway transports.

Operation 1, Mission 2: Destroy SCUD Convoys

Mission Briefing: Destroy SCUD convoys. Steiner is moving missile vehicles through an operation area in preparation for an attack. Sweep the area and destroy the Steiner launch vehicles. The vehicles will be accompanied by an escort, which may include enemy 'Mech forces.

MechLab

Since you only encountered enemy vehicles and tanks in the first mission, you weren't able to salvage any enemy 'Mechs. Thus, you only have one choice this time around. Again select the Shadow Cat from the 'Mech menu. Just as you may have done in the first mission, you can head to the MechLab and customize the Shadow Cat's armor layout.

The stakes are a bit higher for this mission. Along with a collection of enemy vehicles, including Vedettes and SRM Carriers, you'll face off against your first and second enemy BattleMechs. Both are light 'Mechs, however, and you'll have one (uncontrollable) lancemate along for the ride to make things a little easier. The targeting and weapon grouping practice you gained from the first mission should serve you well here.

Battle Plan

Objectives: Destroy all enemies at NAV Alpha. Destroy all enemies at NAV Beta.

Omega Control relays your mission objective: locate and destroy the SCUD mobile missile launchers currently in convoy formation somewhere in the ravine. Maintain active radar and patrol the NAV points (NAV Alpha and NAV Beta) to intercept Steiner's convoy. You have one lancemate for the mission, Gonzalez, who begins slightly ahead of your starting position.

Accelerate your 'Mech to top speed and ready your weaponry. Regroup your weapons to desired presets and prepare for your first combat encounter with an enemy 'Mech—an Osiris light model. Gonzalez will remain ahead of your position and will be the first to spot the foe. The Osiris will be found waiting in the ravine, just before NAV Alpha.

Gonzalez announces he has a visual on an enemy 'Mech and orders you ahead to take it down (see Figure 5.3).

This first battle against a live enemy 'Mech shouldn't be too tough with the help of Gonzalez. Maintain your distance from the enemy Osiris, and aim your laser and missile weapons for its legs. Gonzalez should also circle and attack the 'Mech with his own lasers and

You'll encounter a light enemy 'Mech before you reach NAV Alpha.

missiles. Avoid shooting Gonzalez (he'll spout off a verbal warning if you strike his 'Mech with weapons fire!) by monitoring your radar. If you notice your ally moving into your line of fire, avoid shooting him by strafing to the opposite side.

Though you don't need to rush the enemy 'Mech's destruction, remember that the SCUD convoy will continue to move slowly away from the first NAV point as you do battle. Balance taking your time—and scoring consistent, punishing blows—with blasting away as quickly as you can. Like the first mission, this one takes place on a moon where monitoring your BattleMech's heat output isn't critical to mission success. Once the enemy Osiris has been destroyed, resume course toward NAV Alpha.

NOTE

This mission doesn't offer much in the way of exploration. Following the ravine will get you to the NAV points and objectives in no time. Don't bother attempting to ascend the rocky hills and small mountains that flank the ravine; it's easier to complete the mission if you just stay in the ravine and approach each NAV point in sequence.

Accelerate your 'Mech to top speed and head toward NAV Alpha. Red enemy blips will appear on your radar as you approach. Cycle through these targets to locate one part of the enemy SCUD convoy. This portion of the convoy includes one SCUD mobile launcher, Humvees, hostile Vedette tanks, and a few miscellaneous vehicles.

You're much faster than the SCUD launcher. When you reach the convoy, ignore the SCUD for the moment and concentrate instead on the Vedettes. Target the nearest enemy vehicle and blast away with your lasers; it might require a couple of passes to destroy the lightly armored vehicles. Ramming them should also prove effective.

Switch targets to your first objective, the SCUD launcher, only after all other vehicles have been destroyed (see Figure 5.4). Annihilate the SCUD and prepare to move to the next NAV point.

Select NAV Beta and head toward it using the directional finder on your 'Mech's head-up display. NAV Beta is the location of the second portion of the SCUD

Figure 5.4

A group of Vedettes and Humvees follow the SCUDs.

convoy. Red enemy blips appear on your radar once you near this point. You'll find the second SCUD mobile launcher among this second convoy group. Once again, you'll also encounter several other vehicles, including SRM Carriers and artillery loaders. Destroy the loaders from long range. Avoid being too close when these vehicles explode—the explosion could damage your 'Mech!

Target the vehicles first—once you approach, the SCUD launcher won't escape your wrath. Destroy each enemy in turn with your lasers. This should be sufficient to eliminate the lightly armored foes. Turn your crosshairs on the second SCUD mobile launcher once all vehicles have been cleared. Destroy it with your weaponry.

A final enemy 'Mech, another Osiris, will also enter the battle at NAV Beta. If possible, destroy the vehicles and SCUD mobile launcher before moving against the light 'Mech. Once again, Gonzalez should offer sufficient support against this relatively weak opponent. Avoid shooting Gonzalez and finish off the enemy 'Mech. Its destruction will conclude the mission with complete success.

alternate solution

Should you desire a quick completion of this mission, zoom past the light enemy 'Mech found at NAV Alpha and head straight for the two SCUD convoys. Gonzalez should occupy the first Osiris, and if the enemy light 'Mech decides to follow, your lancemate will continue to fire his weapons against the foe's rear armor. Take out the SCUD mobile launchers and vehicles first, saving the light enemy 'Mechs for later. Rushing through the mission, though, could force you to face off against two light Osiris enemy 'Mechs (the one from NAV Alpha and the other from NAV Beta) at the same time.

Operation 1, Mission 3: Dropship Hunt

Mission Briefing: Destroy Steiner dropships. We have an opportunity to cripple Steiner's activities on and around Kentares IV. Three dropships are preparing for takeoff. If we strike quickly, we can deliver a decisive blow. Be careful if they get powered up; dropships can be devastating. Target the mobile APUs to slow down their launch procedure.

MechLab

Speed certainly helps in this mission against the clock, but so does equipping a 'Mech with the most powerful weapons available. Choose firepower over speed. You won't lose much time when traveling from waypoint to waypoint. Just remember that taking too long to destroy the dropships could jeopardize mission success.

Select your favorite available 'Mech (you should have new selections thanks to last mission's salvage efforts) and equip it with the best weapons available for its slots. Medium and Small Lasers work well against the APUs, but you'll want Large or Pulse Lasers for use against the dropships. Save ammo-based weaponry for the dropships, and group lasers for use against the APUs and base defenses.

Battle Plan

Objectives: Destroy all Steiner dropships. Destroy all mobile APUs.

You begin the mission just outside Steiner's three dropships. Each is parked on a landing pad and surrounded by three APUs. Destroying the APUs slows down the dropship's power-up procedure and damages the dropship as the APUs explode when killed. If allowed to power up, the dropship can activate weapons (which are extremely powerful) and then its engines to initiate launch. A small intel group moves ahead of your position and enters the base to gain recon on the static and mobile defenses that are protecting the dropships and APUs. You're also joined by a lancemate, though he's uncontrollable for the duration of the mission.

Accelerate your 'Mech to top speed and move forward. Automatically target the nearest dropship pad and one of its APUs. Align the target in your crosshairs and approach. The dropships are placed at three different NAV points—Alpha, Beta, and Gamma—inside the base. All three points are visible from each other. You don't have

WARNING

There's no time to hesitate. If a dropship powers up its powerful weapons, the mission becomes much more difficult. And take too long against the APUs, and the dropship will engage its engines and flee the mission area. Stay close to the dropship so its turrets can't fire on you. If you're close, though, when the dropship launches, you can take serious damage.

much time to complete the task before the dropships escape, so go in quickly. Go for the APUs first in order to slow down the launch procedure, and then concentrate on annihilating the dropships. Speed is key!

Once over the rocky hill, the nearest dropship at NAV Alpha appears in your view. Maintain the closest APU as your target and continue to approach. Laser turrets and Vedettes are scattered around the base. Ignore these targets. Allow your lance-mate to deal with the stationary and mobile defenses as you concentrate on the APUs, first at NAV Alpha and then at the other navigation points. As mentioned, there are three APUs at each NAV point. Two lie on the landing platform with another on the ramp. Destroy the APU on the ramp, ascend the ramp, and take out the other two (see Figure 5.5). Alternatively, you could use Jump Jets to leap onto the landing platform. A few blasts with laser weaponry should be sufficient to blow apart each APU.

As soon as the three APUs at NAV Alpha have been destroyed, cycle through targets until you locate an APU at NAV

Destroy the APUs quickly to slow down the dropship's power-up procedure.

Beta, where the second dropship awaits. Adjust your 'Mech's heading and accelerate to top speed. Don't bother descending the landing platform at the ramp; just drop off or use your Jump Jets to leap off. Don't stop to bother with the base defenses as you move to NAV Beta. Twist your torso to fire upon any available targets, but don't slow down or stop your 'Mech. An enemy Osiris 'Mech will also be spotted moving around the base at this point; ignore it as well until the APUs are destroyed.

Take out the APUs at NAV Beta as you did at NAV Alpha. Use Jump Jets to leap up onto the landing platform or simply ascend the ramp, destroying the APU there along the way. If possible, move to the other side of the dropship as soon as possible to escape the base turrets and vehicles' line of fire. Destroying all APUs at NAV Beta triggers a message from command informing you that there are three APUs left around the dropship at NAV Gamma.

Cycle through targets until you're locked onto one of the APUs at NAV Gamma. Drop off the landing platform and move quickly to the final navigation point. Target the APUs here and destroy them as quickly as possible. Finishing off the ninth APU (three at each dropship) completes one mission objective. Unfortunately, you're far from finished! Target NAV Alpha once again and adjust course to intercept. With the APUs out of the way, it's now time to target the dropships themselves. As you move back to the first NAV point, target any turrets, vehicles, or 'Mechs within your view. As you did before, however, don't stop to attack these enemies.

Once you reach NAV Alpha, ascend the ramp onto the landing platform and remain on the other side of the dropship (the opposite side from the center of the base), blocking the base turrets and vehicles' line of fire with the dropship. Target the dropship and start discharging all weapons at it (see Figure 5.6). Don't hold back. As soon as a weapon charges, fire the grouping into the dropship. You may receive various reports from command regarding the power-up condition of the vessels. It's also advisable to back off (set your 'Mech in reverse) after firing on the dropship for a few rounds. Avoid sticking around once the craft explodes, as this explosion could overheat your 'Mech dramatically, forcing a shutdown and costing valuable time.

Eliminating the APUs is only half the battle. Now, target the dropships and prevent them from escaping!

If you're too slow, either with eliminating the APUs or destroying the dropships, one of them might escape. If one does manage to get away, you'll hear orders telling you to remain in the mission area and finish off the remaining two dropships. Destroying these vessels will complete the mission with success. You can't allow two dropships to escape, however, or you're returned to the mission briefing and forced to attempt the task again. The APUs are key to mission success. Destroying them quickly gives you more time to finish off the ships. The mission concludes once you have destroyed all available APUs and enemy dropships.

Operation 1, Mission 4: Base Defense

Mission Briefing: Defending landing facilities. Steiner has taken an increased interest in our activities. We must escape, and you need to provide cover until we can power up our dropships and escape. Make sure the APUs that are powering up the dropship survive. Enemy forces may be heavy and will include 'Mech assets.

MechLab

You won't be moving very much in this mission. Consider a smaller engine in order to free up tonnage for additional ammunition or weaponry. Most action takes place near the friendly landing facilities you're ordered to defend. Missile weaponry will come in handy against the LRM and SRM Carriers that remain back and fire upon the allied dropship from long range. Equip some lasers for the scattered vehicles you'll face, and use missiles or ballistic weaponry against the incoming 'Mechs.

Depending on your salvage efforts from previous missions, you should have several 'Mechs available. The Osiris is a bit too light for use in defending the base, so opt for the Cougar, Shadow Cat, or Hellspawn, depending on their availability.

Battle Plan

Objectives: Defend the APUs while the dropship powers up. Destroy all hostile units to clear for takeoff.

The mission begins with allied command securing cargo vessels in the dropship. Multiple targets have been spotted on radar heading toward the dropship and its vulnerable support units. The primary objective of the mission is to protect the APUs that surround your dropship. As you discovered in the last mission, defending the APUs allows the dropship to successfully charge for launch.

Guarding the APUs is more difficult than expected, largely because they are not all visible at the same time. You can't simply stay on one side of the dropship and protect the APUs on that side, as doing so will leave the other side vulnerable to attack. Therefore, you must continually monitor your BattleMech's radar to locate the nearest incoming threat, even if that threat lies on the other side of the dropship. Stay near the front of the dropship so you can quickly move to a threat coming from either flank (see Figure 5.7).

After the opening cutscene, you'll gain control of your 'Mech. Your lancemates have already entered the field and are targeting hostile units. Locate the nearest enemy unit and accelerate your 'Mech to top speed. Although there are several vehicles on the way—including LRM Carriers, SRM Carriers, Bulldogs, and Vedettes—it's to your advantage to target the nearest enemy 'Mech first. There are four incoming enemy 'Mechs; all are lightly armed and armored, though fairly quick. You'll face Osiris, Hellspawn, and Shadow Cat varieties here.

Figure 5.7

Stick close to the friendly dropship and vulnerable APUs.

These are much quicker than the opposing vehicles and will likely reach the friendly APUs first. Don't let an enemy BattleMech approach the dropship unopposed. Locate the nearest enemy 'Mech, likely a light one, and gather all your weapons into a single attack grouping. Fire on this 'Mech, aiming for a leg or the chest. Attacking with all weapons at once is called an *alpha strike* and, since you're on the moon, you shouldn't have to worry about heat

TIP

The LRM and SRM Carriers don't approach the dropship. They remain a good distance back and attack the APUs from there. Return the favor by eschewing a close approach and simply firing Long-Range Missiles or lasers from a distance. Make sure that a base building doesn't obstruct your line of fire, then lock onto the target, and fire the missiles.

management. Follow up this first blast with another and another until you've diverted the 'Mech's attention away from the dropship.

Continue moving through the base seeking the nearest targets. The base buildings and vehicles, which can provide cover in most search-and-destroy missions, will prove to be a hindrance here. All will block your line of fire on incoming 'Mechs and vehicles. As soon as you cycle to a new target, move away from the buildings to gain a direct line of sight on the enemy vehicle or 'Mech you're currently battling. Target the enemy and fire all your weapons, including any missile-based ones. Weakening or even destroying the 'Mech or vehicle from a great distance will save you precious time and allow you to move on to another enemy target more efficiently.

If you wander too far from the dropship, turn around, locate the big vessel on your viewscreen, and head back—especially if it's announced that an APU is taking damage! Though roaming the field allows you to target and destroy enemy targets quickly, the APUs will be in danger if just one slips by.

As mentioned previously, enemy 'Mechs should be your primary targets unless you have clear line of sight on an opposing vehicle and can eliminate this threat with a single shot. As soon as you've crippled one enemy 'Mech (monitor its damage levels on your head-up display), cycle to the next one and engage it. Keep an eye on the dropship and valuable APUs at all times and challenge any enemy 'Mech targeting either vehicle (see Figure 5.8).

To successfully complete the mission, all enemy threats must be destroyed before you lose the three APUs. Once two enemy 'Mechs are down, quickly cycle to the nearest enemy vehicle and intercept it. If possible, gain long-range line of sight on the vehicle by moving away

'Mechs provide the greatest challenge here. Intercept them before tackling the enemy vehicles.

from obstructing buildings and nonmoving vehicles. Attack with long-range weapons; once destroyed, cycle to the next target and engage.

alternate solution

Enemy 'Mechs pose the greatest danger to the APUs. As suggested in the walkthrough, you should pick the heaviest 'Mech available and stock powerful weapons (remember that you won't have to worry much about heat management concerns). However, if you're having trouble intercepting the incoming threats because of your heavy BattleMech's speed, try to use a faster, lighter 'Mech and load it up with Long- or Short-Range Missiles, Large or Medium Lasers, or Autocannons. The 'Mech's increased speed should allow you to enter the battle as soon as possible. Plus, if necessary, you can disengage with an enemy 'Mech and quickly intercept any hostile vehicle targeting the APUs.

chapter 6
operation 2: "early success" missions

Having just narrowly escaped the Kentares IV moon, you arrive on an arctic world to begin a new operation. The missions here represent the first opportunity for you to be responsible for success and failure. Though you will gain the support of controllable lancemates and acquire valuable salvage, the battles here will become much tougher and will require finely honed combat skills.

This chapter includes complete walkthroughs for the four missions that comprise the "Early Success" operation. The light 'Mechs and vehicles that you fought during the first operation make way for greater dangers. Apply skills learned earlier—including targeting, weapon grouping, eliminating multiple targets, and using hills and structures for cover—to successfully survive the threats faced here.

Operation 2, Mission 1: Recon Area

Mission Briefing: We will be making a hot drop and conducting a recon sweep of the surrounding area. Once this is done, it will allow us to land our forces and begin operations on Kentares IV. This will be your first command opportunity.

MechLab

If you salvaged well during the "Optimism" operation, you should have a rather wide selection of light (and perhaps a few near-medium) BattleMechs to choose from for the second operation's first mission. You'll face two Cougar 'Mechs during this mission, as well as Peregrine combat helicopters, Ravens, Bulldogs, and SRM Carriers.

A complementary Cougar should prove effective as your 'Mech here—though you may wish to opt for a heavier ride, perhaps a Hellspawn or Shadow Cat.

The mission offers one lancemate, and you must donate one of your available 'Mechs for lancemate use. Assign the lancemate to the largest available 'Mech, which should be either the Hellspawn or Shadow Cat. The lighter Osiris and Raven 'Mechs are quick, but a little weak offensively and defensively against the enemy Cougars.

Battle Plan

Objectives: Scout NAV points Alpha, Beta, and Gamma. Destroy all combat units encountered.

The entire second operation takes place in a snow-covered landscape. Like other terrain in *MechWarrior 4*, snow affects the performance of BattleMechs and other certain vehicles. Snow terrain is classified as snow that is higher than a 'Mech's ankles but lower than its knees.

Snow has no effect on hover vehicles. However, the top speed of all tracked vehicles is cut in half. Wheeled vehicles are hindered by 75% of their top speed. The effect of snow terrain on BattleMechs is of the most concern to the player. All 'Mechs (regardless of tonnage) receive a 5% penalty to top speed.

You're sent out and ordered to scout all the NAV points. As soon as you gain control of your BattleMech, select NAV Alpha and adjust your position to proceed toward this nearest navigation point. Your first encounter with opposition forces comes as you near NAV Alpha. Expect to run into an enemy light 'Mech (a Raven), three Peregrine attack helicopters (each loaded with STRK2s), and assorted miscellaneous vehicles, including Snowcats and fuel trucks (see Figure 6.1).

Watch out for the Peregrines, combat helicopters that attack from above.

The Peregrines, while troublesome, aren't a significant threat, at least compared to the enemy light 'Mech. If you're taking too much damage from the choppers, retreat from the light 'Mech (by simply putting some distance between you and the enemy) and target the nearest flying annoyance. Adjust your view to the sky; the Peregrine's attack run will fly straight at your BattleMech. Simply line up your crosshairs and fire your lasers (the larger the better). Save your missiles for the 'Mech, as it doesn't take much to send a Peregrine crashing into the snow-covered ground.

After the three Peregrines and the Raven are destroyed, seek out any remaining vehicles near NAV Alpha. You may find some roaming fuel trucks and Snowcats, but all other hostile units should have been cleared. When you reach NAV Alpha, your directional finder automatically switches to NAV point Beta. Begin heading in that direction, but continually cycle through enemy targets to knock off any fuel trucks, Snowcats, or other vehicles that have wandered away from the rest of the pack. Destroying these noncombat units isn't essential, however, to unit success or failure.

> TIP
>
> The snowy landscape is littered with trees. It can be difficult to maintain sight of the enemy 'Mech through all of that foliage. Don't hesitate to annihilate the trees with your laser weapons or simply run them over with your much sturdier 'Mech. Don't expect the forest to provide the same sort of cover as a solid structure or hill.

Another light 'Mech, a Cougar, will appear on radar as you approach NAV Beta. Do battle against the enemy Cougar and continue moving toward the NAV point. As you reach your destination, you'll notice a small base ahead and receive a communication ordering you to take out the outpost's defenses and all other mobile units in the area. This outpost, a supply depot, lies between NAV Beta and NAV Gamma. All remaining enemy targets can be found within the outpost. Get ready for some target practice!

An additional enemy Cougar will appear on the scope as you enter the outpost. Ignoring the base turrets and other vehicles, deal with the 'Mech right away. Attempt to lead it out of the base so you aren't taking additional fire from the Cougars, Bulldog tanks, and other remaining stationary turrets. After you've finished with the 'Mech, return to the base and cycle through enemy targets. Take out the defensive turrets and each mobile vehicle (see Figure 6.2).

Plenty of targets are scattered around the base. Concentrate on the Bulldogs, Cougars, and LRM and SRM Carriers first; then move to the base turrets, fuel tanks, Snowcats, and other miscellaneous vehicles. A few Peregrines may show up during your assault on the outpost. If this happens, slow your assault and adjust your view to the sky. Line up your lasers and eliminate the helicopters with a few well-placed shots.

Monitor the mobile units surrounding the outpost and clear out the remaining enemy forces. Destroy all opposition forces within the outpost and around the neighboring NAV points Beta and Gamma to conclude the mission with success.

Figure 6.2

Rampage through the enemy outpost, but avoid standing too close to the fuel trucks when they explode!

WARNING

The greatest danger you face after the enemy 'Mechs and hostile vehicles have been destroyed is standing too close to a fuel truck or building explosion. Nothing overheats your 'Mech faster than standing within a fiery explosion! Shoot the fuel trucks from a distance and avoid this dangerous splash effect.

Operation 2, Mission 2: Raid Depot

Mission Briefing: We have located a Steiner base. With a quick strike, we think we can cut off their communications and take control of the base. This will give us some good quality salvage. Enemy resistance will be heavy. Expect 'Mechs supported by combat helicopters.

MechLab

The enemies in this mission run the gamut from powerful stationary Calliope long-range turrets to Peregrine combat helicopters to light-to-medium 'Mechs, including (potentially) a Hellspawn, Catapult (classified as a heavy 'Mech), Cougar, and Shadow Cat. Plus, in order to keep the enemy from reinforcing the supply depot, you must destroy the communications relay before you're detected or else face a tougher path to mission success.

The enemy BattleMechs you'll encounter here are extremely dangerous. Select the heaviest 'Mech available for yourself, and be sure to maximize its firepower potential. Scan the available 'Mechs for Autocannon availability; these powerful ballistic weapons can rip off limbs and tear right through enemy armor. You'll need to take out a communications station before dealing with the enemy 'Mechs, so be sure to equip your 'Mech with Autocannons or missiles in order to level this base quickly. Outfit your lancemate with the next heaviest available 'Mech. Speed isn't critical in this mission. Stay away from the lightest 'Mechs unless you're looking for a tough fight.

Battle Plan

Objectives: Destroy main base defenders. Destroy communications station before they radio for help.

As the mission begins, you're told that a communications relay lies at NAV point Alpha. You begin just out of radar range from the station. If you're spotted by the relay, the enemy will send additional reinforcements to the supply depot, which lies further down at NAV Epsilon. To prevent enemy forces from reinforcing the supply depot defenses, you must destroy the communications relay without being detected by radar. You're instructed to switch on passive radar to approach the communications relay undetected.

> **NOTE**
>
> A Mobile Field Base lies at the map's start position. Should you need to repair or replenish ammo after taking out the communications relay (or at any time during the mission), head back to this location and enter the bay to load up.

Activate passive radar (default control is Ctrl+R) and adjust your heading toward NAV Alpha. Order your lancemate to enter formation. The communications relay station lies in a small clearing just beyond a slight hill and thick forest. If you're detected, you receive a message that the enemy has sent additional reinforcements to the supply depot. If this happens, expect a much different mission. Proceed to the "Alternate Objectives" heading at the end of this mission walkthrough for the suggested solution.

In order to prevent the enemy reinforcements from causing serious damage, maintain position at least 250 meters beyond the communications relay. Fire all weapons and repeat as soon as they have recharged. You must destroy the relay station as soon as possible (see Figure 6.3). Fire quickly—even if you remain 250 meters from the relay station, you will still be detected if you aren't fast enough with your weaponry. With passive sensors active, the communications relay will "notice" you at 250 meters. It will also be alerted if you fire at it. When the station is aware of your presence, you have a limited amount of time to destroy it before the priority message is sent out. You have a tough battle ahead at the supply depot, so attempt to minimize your damage here. Stay away from

Figure 6.3

Destroy the communications relay to make your job at the supply depot much easier.

explosions, and avoid ramming any vehicles and buildings to keep your 'Mech in optimum shape. If you fail to destroy the communications station in time, proceed to the "Alternate Objectives" heading later in this mission walkthrough for the corresponding battle plan.

Follow the NAV points (from Alpha to Beta all the way to Epsilon) and eliminate any enemy patrols before heading to the supply depot. Your eventual goal lies at NAV Epsilon. You'll encounter a wing of Peregrines at NAV Beta. Keep passive radar active, and it's unlikely you will be detected. Continue through the NAV points until you reach Delta and the mountain path to the supply depot at Epsilon.

When you're near NAV Epsilon, toggle it in your directional finder and begin moving toward this critical point. You'll notice several defensive turret emplacements surrounding the supply depot to the right and the left (on a mountain face). If possible, destroy these turrets as you approach. You'll be dealing with 'Mechs and Peregrines when you enter the depot, so you don't want to worry about taking any additional enemy fire. Alternatively, you can keep the mountains between your 'Mech and the Calliope turrets, then attack them from close range upon reaching a good position.

> **TIP**
> The defensive turrets here can strike from a good distance. Equip your 'Mech with long-range lasers and missiles in order to eliminate the turrets from a comfortable location. Knocking out the turrets before entering the supply depot will save you from taking unnecessary damage.

Expect to encounter two enemy 'Mechs (a Cougar and Catapult) as well as a wing of Peregrine combat helicopters. Move away from the 'Mechs to deal with the Peregrines. Attempting to adjust your view and fire on the aerial foes while under attack from an enemy 'Mech could prove disastrous. It's difficult to hit the Peregrines on the move, and if you're standing still, you're an easy target for an enemy 'Mech's lasers and missiles. Back away from the opposing 'Mechs and knock out the Peregrines with a few laser blasts.

After the air units are downed, turn your attention to the enemy 'Mech forces (which could include a nearby patrolling Hellspawn and Shadow Cat called in by the secondary communications station just outside the supply depot). Several structures in the area will serve well as cover against enemy attack. If you're struggling in the battle, take shelter behind one of these buildings and allow the enemy 'Mech to come to you. When the foe enters your line of sight, perform an alpha strike at the

> **TIP**
> You'll find enemy Mobile Field Bases behind the supply depot. Retreat there during the battle and use the bays to repair and rearm your 'Mech. Locating and using the bays could mean the difference between success and failure in this tough mission. Also you will notice possible salvage near the repair bays: a pair of shutdown 'Mechs. Be sure not to shoot these valuable commodities.

BattleMech's most heavily damaged area.

Maintain an awareness of all enemy units. If you've moved far away from an enemy 'Mech, consider cycling through enemy targets to make sure there are no more aerial units in the area or any nearby vehicles taking potshots at your 'Mech (see Figure 6.4). Ignore an enemy 'Mech for a moment if you have a clear shot at a nearby vehicle or remaining Peregrine.

Figure 6.4

Be aware of the enemy as you approach the supply depot—expect to encounter 'Mechs, turrets, vehicles, and air units!

You're after the cargo helicopters in the supply depot. When you've cleared out the enemy presence here, the mission concludes in success. Keep in mind that if you failed to disable the communications relay in time, you'll face a much tougher battle at the supply depot. If you're up against the reinforcements as well, you must minimize damage to your 'Mech in order to survive subsequent battles. Approach the depot slowly and eliminate air units and turrets first. Then move closer and attempt to tackle no more than one or two enemy 'Mechs at a time. Don't get overwhelmed, or you could find yourself ejecting from a flaming hunk of metal.

Alternate Objectives: Ensure allied Swiftwinds arrive and cargo helicopters escape to NAV Zeta. Destroy any assets helpful to Steiner. Break contact with all enemy units.

Failing to knock out the communications station before it sends the priority message introduces a new set of mission objectives. Capturing the base now is out of the question. New orders are to protect incoming Swiftwinds (loaded with pilots), which will park near the enemy cargo helicopters. The pilots will exit the Swiftwinds and board the enemy cargo helicopters and proceed to the escape point at NAV Zeta.

Adjust heading immediately to the enemy base (NAV Epsilon) and order your lancemate to proceed to your selected NAV point or to assume formation beside your BattleMech. Knock out the Calliope turrets as you approach. Locate the cargo helicopters and protect the position. Peregrine combat helicopters are a significant threat to the incoming Swiftwinds. Eliminate the Peregrines quickly; order your lancemate to assist in the attack on the air units.

Incoming enemy 'Mechs will arrive quickly as well. Make sure all Peregrines are destroyed before concentrating on the BattleMechs. The cargo helicopters launch once the pilots board. Escort the choppers to NAV point Zeta. Continue firing on all pursuing enemy 'Mechs. Destroy targets of opportunity, including various base structures, as you proceed to the escape point and finish the revamped mission goals. You won't receive as much salvage for completing this alternate objective. Destroying the communications station early in the mission offers the best and most profitable path through the mission.

Alternate Solution

To prevent additional enemy 'Mechs from reaching the supply depot, knock out the secondary communications facility (it looks like a small radar) just outside the supply depot. If you take too long to eliminate the current 'Mech presence, and you fail to destroy the communications relay at NAV Alpha and the secondary communications facility at the supply depot, tough enemy 'Mechs will arrive and completing the mission becomes significantly more difficult. Knock out all enemy communications bases to prevent reinforcements from arriving. The best way to do this is to proceed forward from NAV Delta until you approach the mission boundary. Run parallel along the path to NAV Epsilon and enter the supply depot from the rear. Locate the secondary communications facility and knock it out from long range with Large Lasers or LRMs. Also destroy the adjacent turret control tower. Locate the Cougar and Catapult near the communications facility. Both are in shutdown mode but will activate after you've destroyed these enemy structures. Don't wait for them to activate. Fire on the Cougar quickly and eliminate the light 'Mech before it has a chance to switch on. Facing just the Catapult provides a major advantage for you and your lancemate.

Operation 2, Mission 3: Escort Techs

Mission Briefing: A group of technicians is pinned down by enemy units. We need to rendezvous with them and escort them to friendly territory. Time is of the essence. The vehicles that the techs are using are very vulnerable, so mind them.

MechLab

Tanks, turrets, and Peregrines dominate the early portion of this escort mission. Long-range Large Lasers will assist in the enemy vehicles' quick destruction (offering one-shot kills of the troublesome Peregrines). Medium 'Mechs (with a few small Ravens) can be found at the beginning and end of the mission. You'll need plenty of firepower to combat the aggressive enemy forces.

Escort the technicians while at the controls of a Hellspawn or Shadow Cat 'Mech, depending on personal preference. Choose larger 'Mechs (in both armor and firepower) if some are available based on mission salvage. If you equip ballistic and missile-based weaponry, conserve your ammunition for use against the enemy 'Mechs guarding the bridge at NAV Beta.

Battle Plan

Objectives: Destroy all turrets at NAV point "Road Block." Link up with the technicians.

You're ordered to proceed to NAV Alpha and join the APCs filled with technicians. Gonzalez is there protecting the technicians until you arrive. NAV Alpha lies due north from your start position. Toggle the navigation point in your directional indicator and order your lancemate to assume formation or proceed to your selected NAV point. Don't trigger the technicians until you have patrolled the area around NAV Alpha and eliminated all enemy threats.

Several enemy units block your path to NAV Alpha, including Humvees (which are nothing more than harmless jeeps you can stomp on), Condors (tanks with Autocannons, lasers, and machine guns), Bulldogs, and an enemy Hellspawn BattleMech. Engage the enemy 'Mech away from the tanks (see Figure 6.5). Order your lancemate to assist in the attack. None of the threats should prove too difficult if you combine firepower with your lancemate. If possible, engage the enemy 'Mech only after you have destroyed the Condors and Bulldogs.

A small roadblock barricade alongside several stationary trailer turrets further bars the way to NAV Alpha and the allied technicians. Finish off any remaining vehicles and the 'Mech before tackling the turrets. Use the hills as cover and fire long-range lasers to destroy the turrets. Be patient and conserve ammunition for use against enemy 'Mechs that will be encountered later in the mission. Order your lancemate against the turrets only after a few are destroyed—you don't want to send in your lancemate too quickly and take fire from the entire turret group. Alternatively, you can also destroy the turret control vehicle nestled amongst the tents north of the turrets. Destroying the turret control vehicle deactivates all turrets!

There's another enemy 'Mech patrolling a small town nearby. This Uziel is a tough customer, boasting PPC

Combat the enemy 'Mech away from the main path to NAV Alpha, especially if you can avoid the Condors' firepower.

laser-based weaponry. If you spot it on your scope, consider destroying this 'Mech before you link up with Gonzalez and the technicians. Alternatively, you can order your lancemate against the Uziel while you remain with the technicians.

Mid-Mission Objectives: Escort the APCs across the bridge to Nav Beta. Destroy the southern bridge.

Approach Gonzalez and the technicians' APCs closely to trigger the next mission objective. You must escort the technicians to NAV point Beta (now available in your directional indicator) and at least two of the three APCs must survive to complete the mission with success. As you begin moving toward NAV Beta, command radios that a bridge stands just before the NAV point. Wait until the APC convoy crosses, then demolish the bridge to complete the mission. If the bridge is destroyed before the technicians cross, the mission can't be completed.

WARNING

Escorting the technicians' APCs to NAV Beta is the critical part of the mission. Eliminate all enemy units you encounter on your way to NAV Alpha to increase your chance of success. Any units left in the area could become troublesome once the APCs have begun their trek to NAV Beta.

Monitor your radar closely. If any enemy units remain (from your trip to NAV Alpha) or any new foes appear on scope, intercept them immediately. The APCs are extremely weak and can't withstand any sort of assault. Follow the transports closely and engage any new incoming targets as soon as they show up on your scope. You can also choose to keep your lancemate near the APCs. Assign him targets as they approach while you explore ahead and engage enemy 'Mechs and vehicles before they threaten the technicians (see Figure 6.6).

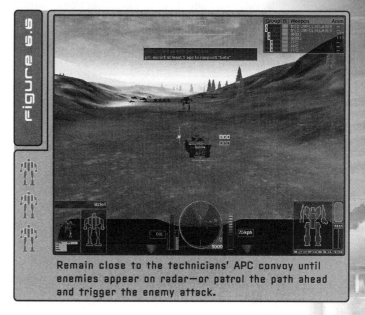

Remain close to the technicians' APC convoy until enemies appear on radar—or patrol the path ahead and trigger the enemy attack.

Enemy Hellspawn 'Mechs will soon approach from the path to NAV point Beta. Peregrine combat helicopters also join in the fun. Though weak units against your 'Mech, the Peregrines are actually quite a threat to the APCs. Order your lancemate to handle the incoming choppers and join in the APCs' defense. It doesn't take many blasts to down a Peregrine, but it's difficult to stop and line up your shot with enemy 'Mechs roaming the area. Clear out the Peregrines and keep your lancemate defending the APCs against anything that gets through. Patrol ahead along the path to NAV Beta.

The first batch of Peregrines, Hellspawn 'Mechs, and SRM Carriers isn't the only danger—a second enemy force arrives as you near NAV Beta. Another Uziel attacks along with a light Raven

TIP

Look for a Mobile Field Base near the second enemy Hellspawn. Once nearby enemy threats are destroyed, use the Mobile Field Base to repair and rearm your BattleMech. This should prepare you well for the mission's final encounter near the southern bridge.

'Mech, a Cougar, and additional SRM Carriers. Stomp out the carriers as quickly as possible (or use long-range lasers) and order your lancemate against the Uziel. Crush the Raven by aiming at its head and midsection. Engage the remaining 'Mechs (the Uziel and Cougar) and keep them away from the technicians' APCs. As soon as the remaining APCs cross to NAV Beta, proceed toward the bridge. Cross it yourself and destroy the bridge behind you to successfully complete the mission.

Operation 2, Mission 4: Capture Base

Mission Briefing: We have an opportunity to strike at Steiner, drive his forces out of the region, and get a little revenge. An added bonus will be the capture of their launch facility and satellite control. The war is starting to turn, let's make this count.

MechLab

This mission includes a mixture of light Cougar and medium Argus and Bushwacker 'Mechs as well as an assortment of vehicles, helicopters, and stationary defensive emplacements. Durability and firepower take precedence over speed. Don't shy away from ammo-based weapons, such as missiles and ballistics, because there's a 'Mech Ammunition Bay inside the enemy base.

The Uziel medium 'Mech (if salvaged from the previous mission) offers a solid mix of durability and firepower from its twin PPCs. Its PPC weaponry, however, is both the Uziel's high and low point. While the weapons boast high damage potential, they recharge slowly and drive 'Mech heat levels up significantly. Furthermore, the Uziel can't hold many more weapons beyond the PPCs. Should you select another 'Mech, place Large Lasers, Autocannons, and missile-based weaponry at top priority.

Battle Plan

Objective: Clear the way to the control center at NAV Beta for your technicians.

You begin the mission just outside the enemy base. Several APCs lie behind you containing the technicians rescued in the previous mission. These transports will proceed into the facility after you've eliminated both the defenders along the outskirts and those found inside the base. When you gain control of your 'Mech, target the nearest enemy, which should be a laser turret, SRM Carrier, or fuel truck just ahead of your current position.

Destroy the fuel truck, even though the unit isn't hostile. The resulting explosion's splash effect should damage the nearby turret and potentially the SRM Carriers patrolling at the edge of the base (if they're close enough). Knock out the two laser cannons and the SRM carriers from long range; don't approach or you'll trigger one of two enemy 'Mechs (an Argus and an Uziel) and have to battle the 'Mechs, the vehicles, and the turrets at the same time.

Remain on the fringes of the base when dealing with the enemy 'Mechs, either both or one at a time (see Figure 6.7). In doing so, you will prevent additional enemies from joining the battle and avoid fire from two long-range Calliope turrets that lie inside the base. Furthermore, ample cover can be found along the outskirts of the base. Several structures outside the front gate can be used as temporary shields against enemy fire. The rocky hills on either side of the path into the base can be used for additional cover or to momentarily flee from a 'Mech.

Maintain sight of the friendly transports and make sure they aren't under fire from

> **TIP**
>
> Autocannons are extremely powerful weapons but also carry limited ammunition. You should limit your use of Autocannons when battling the 'Mechs along the outskirts of the base. Don't waste ammo against the vehicles or turrets, either. You'll face additional 'Mech opposition inside the base, and possessing an ample load of Autocannon rounds will make the battle much easier.

Figure 6.7

Tackle the forces defending the outskirts of the base before proceeding through the front gate.

any rogue enemy vehicles or remaining turrets. Clear out all vehicles and turrets before moving against the enemy 'Mechs. As always, attempt to take on the 'Mechs one at a time to minimize damage. You're going to face additional opposition inside the base, so you need to minimize harm to your BattleMech and maximize the hit ratio to conserve ammunition. Wait for clear shots and monitor the enemy 'Mechs' damage levels so you can target heavily battered areas. Order your lancemate against one 'Mech while you work quickly to destroy the other.

Move inside only after you've cleared the exterior of the base. Enter through the front gate. Proceed slowly, as an additional enemy Uziel waits just inside. Be cautious. Use buildings as cover so you aren't taking fire from the long-range Calliope turrets. When your lancemate is engaged in combat with the enemy Uziel, move against these emplacements. Annihilate them from long range with missiles or Large Lasers.

Adjust your speed to escape around buildings. Double-back and perform an alpha strike on a 'Mech's leg or weakened area to dispose of the foe quickly. The control center lies beyond the front gate behind the two defensive gun turrets (see Figure 6.8). Destroy the enemy 'Mech and turrets before approaching the control center, or you will trigger the allied transports to

Figure 6.8

Make your way into the base to capture the control center.

enter the base—not a good idea with opposing forces still lurking about! Walk up to the control center when the coast is clear to signal the technicians that it's safe for them to enter the base. The technicians will enter the fight after a certain number of enemy units are destroyed—usually everything except the final two Calliope turrets.

Mid-Mission Objective: Defend control center and technicians.

As soon as the technicians reach the control center, the second portion of the mission begins. You're now ordered to defend the now friendly control center and your technicians from an enemy counterattack. Enemy units are inbound within moments. Look to the sky initially and take out the Peregrine combat helicopters that approach. Order your lancemate to assist against the Peregrines. Remember, you need to keep the helicopters' missile fire off the control center and vulnerable technician APCs.

TIP

To the east of the control center are 'Mech Repair and Ammunition Bays. Enter these bays after all base defenses are destroyed to repair and reload your 'Mech in preparation for the enemy counterattack. Rearming your 'Mech will carry even more importance if you're equipped with ballistic (specifically Autocannons) and missile-based weaponry.

A large group of enemy 'Mechs (including Cougar and Argus models) and a squad of LRM Carriers approach the base soon after the combat helicopters have been destroyed. Target the LRM Carriers and blast them quickly with long-range lasers. Order your lancemate against the nearest Cougar. The enemy Argus 'Mechs offer a much tougher challenge. Keep the fight away from the control center and close to the base entrance. Monitor your radar closely as some Cougars will attempt to flank your position and attack the control center and technicians from the west. As soon as the enemy units are destroyed and the technicians complete their job inside the control center, the mission concludes in success.

alternate solution

Instead of combating the defending 'Mechs alone in the open, use the base environment to your advantage. Lure enemy 'Mechs to the launch facilities and blast the missile on the launch pad. The resulting explosion provides a secondary method of damaging opposing units. Make sure that you're well away from the launch facility when it goes up in flames. Save these explosions for the counterattack against the technicians to further ensure their survival.

This mission also has additional "hidden" secrets for you to uncover:

- There are four smaller bases where some enemy forces are shut down (these comprise the counterattack 'Mech groups). You may want to attack the two Cougars in the upper left (near the Repair Bays) and the two Peregrines in the upper right, though the combat helicopters pose very little threat. Also the four late-arriving LRM Carriers are located to the bottom right of the main base.

- There is a turret control tower to the left and behind the control center. If you destroy this tower before you take out the two Calliope turrets that guard the control center, your technicians will switch the Calliopes back online and use them in the installation's defense against the enemy counterattack.

- Don't underestimate the power of the friendly Bulldog tank. This unit is a pretty good shot and will provide extra firepower during installation defense.

operation 3: "First command" missions

The operation "First Command" shifts from the snow-covered world to an alpine land-scape. Dense trees and rocky hills dominate the mission layouts. Since you've lost the environmental advantages of the moon and the cold weather, you must now start man-aging your BattleMech's heat level. Thankfully, the presence of a few mountain lakes provides an occasional reprieve. Plus, the rocky alpine hills serve as nice cover and as potential escape routes and ambush points against enemy units.

This chapter includes complete walkthroughs for the three missions that comprise the "First Command" operation. Battles are getting tougher, and each expedition requires more concentration. Coordination with your lancemates is also needed; it's difficult to win these battles all by yourself. Rely on your allies to tackle some targets for you. Conserving ammunition and firing accurate shots will pay dividends. Be pre-pared to face multiple enemies at the same time; the faster you can eliminate these foes, the easier each battle becomes.

Operation 3, Mission 1: Destroy Patrols

Mission Briefing: Destroy patrols. A Steiner dropship has crashed, and we may have a chance to capture it and further cripple their ability to move troops. Scout the nearby area and brush aside the enemy screen.

MechLab

'Mechs form the only enemy target in this patrol mission. Long-range lasers and missiles can help get early hits on approaching foes, but powerful short-range weapons will provide the most important advantage against the opposing units.

If you favor laser-based weaponry, consider choosing the Uziel and its twin PPCs as your 'Mech here. Several lakes in the area can help keep your BattleMech's heat down, and you won't have to worry about lacking ammunition. Select the Argus (if salvaged from the previous mission) if you desire ballistic-based weaponry and Autocannons. Be careful to conserve ballistic ammunition, though—nine enemy 'Mechs will be encountered during your patrol.

Battle Plan

Objectives: Destroy all units at NAV points Alpha, Beta, Gamma, and Delta.

Prepare yourself for a challenging mission. The only objective in this mission is to destroy the opposition. There's no depot to raid or control center to capture—it's kill or be killed! You're ordered to patrol the NAV points and eliminate all enemy patrols encountered.

Easy enough guidelines to follow? Not exactly. A total of nine enemy 'Mechs will be faced during the course of this mission. While none is especially tough (Cougars and Osiris models will form most of the enemy contingent), the gauntlet of battles will test all of your combat skills. You must minimize damage to your own 'Mech while maximizing ammo usage and effectiveness (should you be equipped with ballistic or missile weapons). Enemies must be taken out quickly so you aren't enduring extended fire from multiple 'Mechs at any given time.

Because you must destroy so many enemy 'Mechs to complete the mission, you need to conserve ammunition or consider avoiding ballistic and missile weapons in the MechLab. If you have accuracy troubles, take a majority of laser-based weaponry so you don't eventually become strapped for ammo. If you're equipped with mostly ballistic or missile weapons, firepower problems could emerge when you reach the final few 'Mechs.

Start your 'Mech and increase speed to full. Begin heading to NAV Alpha, your first patrol stop against the enemy 'Mechs, by proceeding toward 300 degrees on the directional finder. You'll emerge over a sizeable hill and spot two Cougars as you near the NAV point (see Figure 7.1). Fire on the Cougars as you approach. Group all of your weapons into a single unit and perform an alpha strike against one or both of the approaching enemy 'Mechs.

Two Cougars appear on radar after you scale the hill leading toward NAV Alpha.

Since you're out in an alpine forest, you don't have significant cover to use against these multiple opponents. Should you need to flee, head over the nearest hill. Move down the incline until the top of your 'Mech lies under the top of the hill. Then turn around and wait until the enemy follows. Keep the nearest 'Mech targeted and, when it appears over the hill, fire an alpha strike at either its legs or a heavily damaged area.

Bait any remaining BattleMechs in the area in a similar fashion to finish them off. If your initial shot fails to cripple a 'Mech, proceed back over a hill and again lure the opponent to the other side. Order your lancemate against one Cougar while you tackle its comrade. After one target has been destroyed, shift your crosshairs to the other enemy Cougar.

You're ordered to NAV Beta as soon as the battle against the Cougars has been concluded. As you approach this spot, two Osiris and one Raven 'Mech (with ECM active) appear on your scope. Both are light 'Mechs and shouldn't pose much of a problem if you can refrain from becoming overwhelmed. Keep your lancemate busy with one of the opponents as you battle the other two. Again, use the landscape to your advantage. Scale hills to escape from multiple opponents. Lure your foes over the hills and gain first strike advantage over these light 'Mechs.

Proceed to NAV Gamma once you've cleared NAV Beta. As you approach this NAV point (which can be reached by either moving around or over the large mountain near NAV Beta), you'll spot a lake. Two enemy Vulture 'Mechs appear on radar as you approach this body of water; you'll spot them closing on your position from just beyond the lake. Once again, use the nearby hills to your advantage. Attempt to separate the 'Mechs and gain easy hits by luring each over a hilltop.

You can also use other landscape features to your advantage. Take a swim in the lake and fire upon the enemy from there. The shallow water improves the efficiency of heat sinks, allowing you to fire off your laser-based weapons aggressively and often (see Figure 7.2). In deeper water—water that rises up between a BattleMech's ankles—a Mech's top speed is reduced, though heat sinks work even more efficiently.

NAV point Delta, which also lies adjacent to a small lake, is your final destination in this mission; proceed there once you've cleared the Vultures at NAV Gamma. Once you've arrived, you'll find an Osiris and a Cougar on patrol looking for a fight. The hills on your right should be used for cover if you need to flee the battle at some point. Hide beyond the hill and wait for the 'Mechs to approach. When they do, hammer them with alpha strikes. If you're relatively undamaged, stay in the lake to the left and fire upon the light 'Mechs from there. The mission ends in success once you've cleared all navigation points of enemy patrols.

WARNING

If you happen to run out of ammo or your lasers are destroyed, alternate means need to be employed to finish off the enemy. Order your lancemate against the enemy while you retreat or, if you're in a heavier 'Mech, use ramming techniques. Pummeling an enemy into submission is even easier if you have Jump Jets and know how to perform the death from above maneuver (see Chapter 2: Combat Tactics 101).

Figure 7.2

Don't hesitate to lead enemy 'Mechs into the nearby lake.

Operation 3, Mission 2: Capture Convoy

Mission Briefing: Capture convoy. Steiner is attempting to move repair supplies, technicians, and reinforcements to their dropship. Intercept the convoy, destroy the military forces, and capture the convoy. They are ahead of you on the mountain pass, so move fast.

MechLab

You should have a wide selection of light and medium 'Mechs available in the MechLab. The versatile Vulture, if salvaged from the previous mission, should prove effective with its Large Lasers and Long-Range Missiles. But, if you still possess an intact Uziel or Argus, consider using one of these medium 'Mechs and their PPC and Autocannon weaponry, respectively.

Outfit your lancemate in a Vulture, Uziel, or Argus—whichever is available and you don't choose for yourself. If you'd rather not risk losing one of these 'Mechs, place your lancemate inside a Shadow Cat or a Hellspawn.

Battle Plan

Objectives: Overtake the enemy convoy and destroy its guards. Destroy all Steiner forces.

You begin the mission in a mountain pass. Large hills and lush forestry surround your position. You're told that the enemy convoy lies near NAV point Alpha, already activated on your head-up display. Orders are to locate the convoy and destroy its escorts. With the escorts down, the convoy is expected to surrender control to you and your lancemates. Accelerate your 'Mech forward and order your lancemates to assume formation.

> TIP
>
> There are two major routes to NAV point Alpha. You can ascend the tall mountains surrounding the path and cut through the forest, or you can follow the mountain path around and through the hills. It's not a direct route but it's a flatter one. Stick to the mountain path. It provides a better attack angle on the convoy escort, and it's much easier to move on flat ground than over steep hills.

Enemy Nightshades appear on radar almost immediately. Target these air units (three will pass over) as they approach from behind your starting position. Order your lancemates to attack as well in case you miss the targets. Fire only laser-based weaponry at the Nightshades; don't waste missiles or ballistics ammunition (see Figure 7.3). Destroy all three and continue to NAV point Alpha, either directly across the mountains or indirectly by staying on the flat mountain pass. The Nightshades do not want to fight, so let them go if

Shoot down the enemy Nightshades with lasers to save ammo for use against the convoy's escort.

they make a run for it. The trek to the convoy shouldn't take long.

As you make your way toward NAV Alpha, the convoy will appear on radar. Guarding the convoy are a lance of enemy 'Mechs and a squad of Bulldog tanks. Among the 'Mechs are two Cougars, an Argus, and a Vulture. If you stopped your BattleMech, you'll realize that the convoy is on the move from left to right (based on your trajectory toward NAV Alpha). Approach its rear but stay hidden by the small, rolling hills and scattered trees. Avoid emerging into view of the tanks and the accompanying 'Mechs.

As you near the convoy, peek over the hill (keeping your lancemates in formation) and fire on the nearest enemy 'Mech. Lure that foe and as many of his fellows as possible into an ambush. As the first enemy 'Mech emerges over the hill, fire all weapons in an alpha strike at its leg or head area. Then order both lancemates to attack this early arrival. You've likely attracted the attention of all convoy escorts by this time. Keep your lancemates occupied with a single enemy as you engage the Cougars. These light 'Mechs should fall quickly. Use the nearby hills and valleys as cover when dueling the other remaining enemies.

The Vulture and Argus 'Mechs offer the greatest challenge. Use lancemates to target one foe while you battle the other or the two light Cougars (see Figure 7.4). Monitor your lancemates' opponent carefully; once it's heavily damaged or crippled, assign your allies to a new enemy 'Mech target. Handling the Bulldog tanks shouldn't be too difficult. Stomp on them if possible or fire lasers at them at the first opportunity. Don't worry about the convoy. Though it may keep moving away from your position, you'll be able to catch up. Concentrate on the escorts. Keeping your distance from the convoy also ensures its survival, as stray projectiles won't strike the vehicles.

Order your lancemates to take on the Vulture or Argus while you aggressively attack the other.

Continually monitor your lancemates' target. Assist their battle if necessary by adding your firepower into the mix. Consider ordering the lancemates to attack another 'Mech while you finish off their crippled target. The convoy's escort must be completely destroyed in order to finish the mission—its commanders won't surrender until enemy forces have been eliminated! Catch up with the convoy after completing the initial battle. If any vehicles or 'Mechs remain with the convoy, attack them from long range and avoid firing at or around the vehicles.

NOTE

Be aware of the location of an enemy 'Mech before delivering a killing blow. If the enemy 'Mech is close to the convoy, you may want to wait before firing. If that 'Mech's fusion plant goes critical, the resulting explosion may damage or destroy the convoy.

Operation 3, Mission 3: Destroy Dropship

Mission Briefing: Destroy the dropship. We can take a strike at the Steiner dropship. It is crippled but that does not mean it will not get its weapons online. If it does activate its weapons, use range, mobility, and friendly artillery to bring it down. If we win, we will have a huge advantage over Steiner.

MechLab

You won't face significant opposition until you reach Steiner's dropship. Once there, though, you'll find yourself under fire from vehicles, 'Mechs, and stationary turrets. The Uziel and its powerful PPC weaponry should be able to handle the opposition, though the PPCs' high heat and slow recharge could pose problems in close-quarters combat. The Argus with its Autocannons, missiles, and lasers carries enough firepower and armor to survive, both offensively and defensively.

Two lancemates are available for the mission. Their primary goal is to occupy dropship defensive forces while you destroy vehicles, turrets, and finally the dropship itself. Place them in durable medium 'Mechs with enough offensive weaponry to stand toe to toe with an enemy Argus and Mauler 'Mech. You were awarded a Catapult after Operation 2, Mission 2. Its Long-Range Missiles may prove effective here.

Battle Plan

Objective: Find the damaged Steiner dropship.

Orders are to take out a nearby dropship before it escapes. The trick is that you need to remain out of enemy radar view until you reach the vessel. If you're detected, the dropship begins to power up. Depending on how far away you are when it begins its power-up sequence, you likely won't reach the craft before it lifts off. You're told at the mission's start that the dropship lies northeast of your start position. Power your 'Mech, accelerate to top speed, and adjust your heading to a course in this direction.

A group of enemy 'Mechs will appear on radar soon after you've begun the long trek to the enemy dropship. Don't fire on this patrol; a battle with these 'Mechs takes valuable time that you'll need in order to reach the dropship (see Figure 7.5). Maintain passive radar to avoid detection by the patrol of Cougars.

Instead of engaging the patrol, follow it to the dropship. It's difficult to lose your desired heading. Large mountains lie to the northern and eastern ends of the map. The resulting valley forms a path to the northeast that will eventually lead to the dropship, sitting deep inside a crater. The vessel's crash has created a burnt strip of land. Locate this scarred area, and you'll find the dropship at its end. You may spot additional enemy 'Mech patrols during your rush to this spot. Ignore these patrols and continue your trek toward the damaged, but still functional enemy dropship.

Mid-Mission Objective: Destroy damaged Steiner dropship.

When you near the dropship, you'll soon discover it's not alone. Several Bulldog tanks, Argus and Mauler

You don't have the time to start a battle here.

'Mechs, and defensive turrets protect the critical structure. (The Mauler is powered down behind the dropship. It will power up approximately 90 seconds after you attack the dropship.) Here's where the real battle begins. You learned at the mission's start that you can call on artillery strikes to assist in the dropship's destruc-

tion. Move in on the dropship's defenses and radio for an artillery strike.

The dropship is damaged, but some of its weapons are still functional. Furthermore, the longer the battle takes, the more weapons the dropship can use, as they're currently being repaired (see Figure 7.6). Several

Don't expect much trouble at first, but don't waste time in destroying the dropship!

APUs around the dropship can be destroyed to decrease the vessel's ability to quickly fix its weapons.

Your biggest problem won't be the dropship itself but the surrounding defensive turrets, vehicles, and enemy 'Mechs. Take out vehicles only if a shot becomes available; these units won't require much firepower to destroy, and you can eliminate them while engaged with another target. Order your two lancemates against enemy 'Mechs as you clear out the tanks, APUs, and turrets. Target the dropship as soon as possible and use all your firepower, including the allied artillery strike.

Enemy 'Mechs will pose a greater problem as you can't afford to participate in a drawn-out battle. Not only will you take additional damage from turret, vehicle, and dropship fire, but the longer you take, the faster the APUs will repair the vessel.

While the dropship is weakened, it still carries a large amount of armor plating. Use artillery strikes to weaken the vessel and take frequent shots at it. Keep moving to minimize damage from the surrounding defenses. If you're healthy, consider ramming turret defenses and vehicles while continuing to fire on the dropship or other targets of opportunity. The mission ends in success once the dropship has been destroyed.

operation 4: "building forces" missions

The arid desert sets the stage for Operation 4, "Building Forces." This new landscape brings along its fair share of new problems. Heat management is an even greater issue here. Difficulties begin when you combine bigger 'Mechs and better weapons with unforgiving weather conditions. Counter the hot desert air with additional heat sinks, or monitor your heat gauge closely and be prepared to shut down or flush coolant to survive the dangerous battles ahead.

This chapter includes complete walkthroughs for the six missions that comprise the "Building Forces" campaign. It's time to take the battle to the enemy. The missions here feature some of the toughest battles you've faced thus far. Use your squad of allied units wisely against a horde of opponents or face the consequences of an outnumbered lance. Victory here could turn the tide in this ongoing war.

Operation 4, Mission 1: Raid Base

Mission Briefing: We have the opportunity to raid a large Steiner base as part of a combined arms action. Your job is to guard a convoy of vehicles as they enter the base and loot the supply warehouses. Beware of possible heavy 'Mech forces. Watch for the heat impact of the desert terrain.

MechLab

This is primarily a defensive mission where you must guard the convoy on its way to loot the enemy base. After the raid is complete, you must defend and escort the convoy to the designated extraction point. But, in this case, the best defense is a great offense. You need to attack and keep the enemy presence away from the convoy. A sturdy, heavier 'Mech with long-range weaponry should provide the durability and firepower required for success.

Long-range firepower helps during the initial approach. LRMs or PPCs are good choices. The Catapult, Argus, and Uziel are all solid 'Mechs to pick for this mission. The Argus carries LRMs as well as Autocannons for close-range combat. If you have one available, pilot the Argus yourself and send lancemates out in the Catapult or Uziel. Keep in mind that the Uziel depends heavily on PPC weaponry, which can cause significant overheating problems in the dry desert air.

Battle Plan

Objective: Guard the convoy as it proceeds to and loots the first site.

New radio orders come in as soon as the mission begins. This assignment is a combined effort where several different organized squads must complete specific tasks. A convoy group of transports and tanks will follow your lead into a nearby enemy base in an effort to loot this stronghold of its valuable supplies. Friendly aircraft along with a tank squad on the southern flank will provide a diversionary attack and will hopefully serve as the decoy you'll need to successfully punch into the base. You must escort the convoy into the enemy fortress, providing fire support all the way.

As soon as you gain control of your 'Mech, adjust its heading to NAV Alpha and accelerate. Defensive turret emplacements will be the first enemy units to appear on radar. Charge ahead of the friendly convoy and target the nearest turret. Use Large Lasers to eliminate it. Minimize your damage by remaining just out of range. Back off if you're taking damage (see Figure 8.1). You can't afford to suffer excessive harm this early in the mission, as there's a lot of fighting still to come. If you're moderately or heavily damaged by these turrets, it'll be difficult to eliminate defending 'Mechs and protect the convoy from counterattack.

Follow the road and the bridge into the base. Avoid using the hills and mountains to the left, as taking the road gives you a better angle against the turrets that lie inside the fortification. Once over the bridge, you can employ the enemy buildings as cover against the turret fire. Peek around these structures and eliminate the remaining turrets from long range. If heat becomes a problem, duck out of sight and emerge only when your weapons are charged and ready to resume the attack. Maintaining sight of the

Figure 8.7

Don't attempt to attack the turret emplacements at close range, as shown here.

convoy, keep enemy units and turrets from attacking the more fragile vehicles in it. If the convoy reports that it's under fire, check your radar. Locate the turret or enemy unit responsible and intercept it as quickly as possible.

You're in the desert now—not exactly optimum conditions for a BattleMech. Overheating will become a definite problem here, especially if your 'Mech is equipped with a high number of laser-based weapons. Monitor your 'Mech's heat level closely and flush coolant (defaults to the "F" key) into the system whenever necessary. Many defenders are inside the enemy base. Scout the roads along the outskirts and knock off the SRM Carriers looking to ambush your convoy. As you have done previously, listen for the convoy vehicles to relay their current status. If the convoy comes under attack, intercept the assailants immediately. Target the convoy by cycling through friendly units and then accelerate to top speed. Protecting the convoy is key to completing the mission with success, so make this your first priority at all times.

Enemy 'Mechs (Cougars and Shadow Cats first) can also be found defending within the enemy stronghold. Fuel pods are also scattered around the base. Fire on these pods if an enemy 'Mech walks near them. The explosion and resulting splash effect will inflict damage on the enemy. Of course, this works both ways. Monitor the location of the fuel pods and avoid walking into one or wandering too close when an enemy 'Mech has you under fire. If you're in the blast radius when a pod goes off, you'll take damage and your heat level will soar to an extreme.

The initial 'Mech defenders shouldn't pose much of a problem, especially with such a wealth of cover. Make an effort to keep buildings intact as you're expected to defend the base once the friendly convoy completes its capture. Concentrate on the enemy 'Mechs and use the structures and fuel pods to your advantage (see Figure 8.2). But monitor the convoy's position. Don't fire upon the fuel pods if the convoy happens to be near; the explosion can devastate the convoy and jeopardize (or completely undermine) mission success. Clear out all defending 'Mechs, vehicles, and turrets before ushering the convoy into the base. Eventually the convoy announces its completion of the first objective and moves on to loot the second base site.

note

The decoy tank units on the southern flank can be very useful. The longer the tank squad can stay in the field, the longer they will occupy two enemy BattleMech units—and possibly some of the base's tank assets. The tank squad will let you know when they have to pull out. Listen for this transmission and realize you may have additional enemy units inbound.

Figure 8.2

Terminate the enemy 'Mech defenders as quickly as possible.

Mid-Mission Objective:
Guard the convoy as it proceeds to and loots the second site.

The convoy proceeds ahead to raid the second site. The enemy aggressively sends in new 'Mechs to prevent the raid. Expect to spot incoming Thanatos, Bushwacker, Osiris, and Raven enemy 'Mechs as the convoy makes its way to the second site (and the third site once the second has been looted).

The Osiris and Raven offer easy targets. Handle them yourself and order your lancemates against the tougher Thanatos and Bushwacker. Destroy the Osiris and Raven quickly; don't worry about salvaging these light 'Mechs, which won't be useful additions to your MechLab at this stage of the game.

The Thanatos and Bushwacker are quite powerful, though, and should be salvaged if possible. Once the Osiris and Raven are obliterated, check the Thanatos and Bushwacker to see which has taken more damage. Shift your crosshairs onto the weaker of the two 'Mechs. At some point during the fight, the convoy informs you that the second site has been looted and the convoy is proceeding to the third.

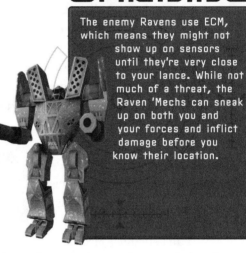

WARNING

The enemy Ravens use ECM, which means they might not show up on sensors until they're very close to your lance. While not much of a threat, the Raven 'Mechs can sneak up on both you and your forces and inflict damage before you know their location.

Mid-Mission Objective: Guard the convoy as it proceeds to and loots the third site.

Continue battling enemy 'Mechs or vehicles, if applicable. Additional enemy 'Mechs won't arrive until the convoy completes its raid. Cycle through the remaining enemy 'Mechs to seek out the most damaged target. Divert fire toward this particular BattleMech in an effort to down the opposition quickly. Eliminate the enemy's numbers as fast as possible. It's to your advantage to take out as many enemy BattleMechs as possible before the convoy finishes its objective. The convoy will send a transmission upon completing the third site objective, ordering you to escort the convoy to the extraction point, which lies at NAV point Epsilon.

Mid-Mission Objective: Proceed to extraction point (NAV Epsilon).

Additional enemy 'Mechs intercept the convoy and your newly captured supplies on the way to the extraction point. Order lancemates against these Uziel and Hellspawn 'Mechs. Stay close to the convoy yourself to intercept attackers as soon as possible. The mission ends in success once the convoy and your 'Mech successfully reach the extraction point at NAV Epsilon. Keep lancemates engaged with enemy 'Mechs. Order them to defend specific convoy units or to assume formation alongside the convoy. Proceed to NAV Epsilon with the convoy and attack pursuing enemy 'Mechs with missiles or long-range lasers (also known as Large Lasers).

alternate solution

You aren't ordered to eliminate all the base defenders—just protect the convoy as all three base sites are looted. Once the convoy starts its march to the extraction point (NAV Epsilon), expect additional enemy 'Mechs to enter and pursue. These late arrivals are best ignored, unless they directly threaten the convoy's path toward NAV Epsilon. Sometimes it's best not to engage and simply follow alongside the convoy until you reach the extraction point. Also, locate the Mobile Field Bases in the area of NAV Beta. Repair and rearm your 'Mech here, but monitor enemy movement closely. Don't leave the convoy unguarded for a long period of time.

Operation 4, Mission 2: Defend Base

Mission Briefing: Steiner's forces are on a major offensive. We need to relieve forces at NAV point Alpha and proceed to a large allied base at NAV point Beta. You can expect a fierce assault by enemy forces at both locations. Again, watch the impact of the desert heat upon your 'Mech.

MechLab

Though at first a defensive task, this mission quickly turns into a challenging 'Mech-to-'Mech battle where the numbers favor the enemy side. Be prepared to tackle numerous opposition 'Mechs. You'll find moderate cover inside the base, although the structures are friendly and need to be protected from enemy fire.

The Vulture, with its long-range lasers and missiles, possesses the firepower to compete against the enemy onslaught. Furthermore, the Vulture's full-range torso twist allows you to adjust the crosshairs to any incoming enemy 'Mech without adjusting your heading. If you prefer Autocannon weaponry, select the Argus, Thanatos, or Bushwacker (if these 'Mechs are available in the MechLab).

You have three lancemates available for this tough mission. Place them inside 'Mechs that complement your own choice. For instance, if you prefer close-range superiority, outfit a lancemate inside a long-range specialist such as the Catapult. Then order this 'Mech to engage long-range enemy targets as soon as you spot them on radar.

Battle Plan

Objectives: Defend 'Mech hangars at the base (NAV point Beta). Get to NAV point Alpha. Eliminate guerrilla 'Mechs.

This is one of the most hectic missions thus far—be prepared to compensate for changing conditions and orders on the spot. You'll need to be quick on your 'Mech's feet and listen carefully to communications from your allies.

Scattered contacts are reported on radar, with Steiner's enemy lance of 'Mechs heading toward the allied base at NAV point Beta. You're ordered to first head to NAV Alpha, where allies will hold the position until you arrive. Long-range radar reports many enemies en route.

Adjust your heading to NAV point Alpha and accelerate your 'Mech to top speed. Enemy Peregrine helicopters will soon appear on your radar. Maintain your speed if possible and adjust your viewpoint to the sky in order to eliminate the hovering Peregrines. Don't waste missile or ballistic ammunition on them; the air units aren't especially strong and can be wiped out with a few shots from laser-based weaponry. Save ballistic and missile ammo for use against the enemy 'Mechs you'll encounter later in the mission—it's much more important to destroy base attackers quickly than to shoot down Peregrines with ballistic weapons or missiles.

Keep moving toward NAV Alpha. Avoid making too many stops to take on the Peregrines. You should be able to adjust your Mech's torso and take out the air units as they approach. As you near the NAV point, enemy 'Mechs (Shadow Cats or Uziels) will begin appearing on your scope. Attack if a battle presents itself (see Figure 8.3), but don't waste too much time engaging in a

Take shots if they're offered, but stay on course to the rendezvous point at NAV Alpha.

deathmatch situation. Fight off the 'Mechs while continuing to make your way to NAV Alpha as quickly as possible. Additional enemy 'Mechs will appear, but, as stated, don't bother pausing to fight. Adjust your course slightly to use the rocky desert hills as cover against any enemy fire against your rear flank.

Mid-Mission Objective: Defend the antiaircraft guns.

As you near NAV point Alpha, a new enemy 'Mech lance of Shadow Cats appears on radar. This group of foes approaches from the canyon and is headed toward the rendezvous position at NAV Alpha. The enemy group also includes SRM Carriers. Target the nearest enemy and engage it immediately. Order lancemates against the Shadow Cats to give you time to deal with the vehicles. The vehicles should fall quickly, especially if you can launch a few laser blasts from long range. Attack the incoming 'Mechs as well; attempt an alpha strike or two to gain an early advantage.

Enemy Shilone bombers fly over in an attempt to destroy the NAV Alpha structures. Adjust your crosshairs to take down the bombers, preferably with laser weaponry. Use lancemates to assist in the destruction of the air units if most of the incoming enemy 'Mech and vehicle group is contained.

Here's where a fast 'Mech comes in handy during this mission. During the assault on the NAV Alpha rendezvous point, the remnants of the enemy BattleMech lance peel off and move toward the allied base at NAV Beta. Because these 'Mechs are light, they're fairly swift and will certainly outrun you if you chose durability and firepower over speed. A fast 'Mech could keep up with the enemy and take potshots against their rear armor, which is typically weaker. You don't want to fall too far behind. If you're in a slower 'Mech, adjust your heading quickly. Try and anticipate the enemy lance's movements before they come. Take out the vehicles with lasers, and then switch to NAV Beta immediately. Anticipate the lance's maneuvering and attack the enemy 'Mechs as they begin their advance to NAV Beta.

Those 'Mechs, as well as others that will approach as you near NAV Beta, are on an assault course against the allied 'Mech hangars. You must defend the hangars from

> TIP
>
> The enemy 'Mechs approaching NAV Alpha quickly change course to spearhead the attack on the allied base at NAV Beta. Listen to radio communications carefully and don't hesitate to divert your attention from current targets to follow the lance of 'Mechs. If enemy vehicles persist in harassing you, blast them from long range as you maneuver away from NAV Alpha.

attack to preserve your ally's ability to produce additional 'Mechs and stay competitive in the ongoing war. Take shots against the enemy lance as you speed toward NAV Beta. If you can weaken the enemy 'Mechs even slightly, the base's defenses will have an easier time holding them off until you arrive. This is especially important if you're in a slower BattleMech and can't arrive at the same time as the enemy group.

The path to NAV Beta ascends a hill and leaves you looking down on the base below. Base defenses should already be engaged with fending off any enemy 'Mechs that managed to survive the trek from NAV Alpha (see Figure 8.4). Friendly fire can be a problem here, so don't haphazardly blast away at enemy 'Mechs. Base structures are weak and won't be able to withstand much firepower. Use the buildings as cover, but don't discharge your weapons without a clear line of sight on the enemy. Maneuver around the buildings and attempt to strike the opposing 'Mechs at close range to avoid dealing damage to your allies.

Figure 8.4

Approach the base at NAV Beta quickly, but avoid inadvertently firing upon friendly structures.

The mission has just begun upon your reaching NAV Beta. Not only do you have the remaining enemy 'Mechs from NAV Alpha to contend with, but an additional lance of four enemy 'Mechs, including Vultures and Uziels, approaches from just beyond the allied base. Allied defenses should be able to handle the remaining NAV Alpha 'Mechs, though you should help your friends out by inflicting as much damage as possible before intercepting the fresh arrivals. Monitor your radar closely and pound on any enemies inside the base before adjusting course to the new 'Mech lance. The mission ends in success when all enemy attackers have been defeated. The 'Mech hangars and the base must survive the assault.

Operation 4, Mission 3: Capture Barges

Mission Briefing: There are a number of barges laden with supplies being moved through our operational area. Steiner will doubtlessly be guarding these barges well, but civilians will be captaining the barges. If you can destroy the barges' escorts, they will surrender, giving us much needed supplies.

MechLab

Speed and long-range weaponry play an important role in this mission to capture munitions barges. You must be quick enough to reach the barges before they enter the safety of NAV Beta. However, long-range weaponry is also important to knock out incoming patrol boats, Peregrine combat helicopters, and the handful of defending 'Mechs.

The Vulture (LRMs and Large Lasers), the Uziel (PPCs), and the Argus (LRMs and Autocannons for 'Mech combat) all include the necessary durability and firepower, though each is limited by only average speed. Send lancemates in Uziel or Argus 'Mechs and have them concentrate on 'Mech-to-'Mech battles, while you move quickly and aggressively through the enemy defenses to capture the barges.

Battle Plan

Objectives: Destroy all armed escorts around the barges. Capture (come within 100 meters) four of the six barges. At least four barges must survive.

The battles aren't especially tough in this mission. Nothing you fight should present much of a problem, especially against the squad of lancemates you're now commanding. This assignment's toughest component is the time restriction. The enemy barges begin ahead of your start position and will continue to move away from you during the course of the mission. As you attempt to approach and capture them, the enemy sends air, water, and 'Mech units on an intercept course. This then becomes a

NOTE

If an enemy unit approaches a captured barge within 100 meters, the barge will be recaptured by the enemy. Keep enemy units away from captured barges or monitor your radar closely. If you notice a blue blip changing red, a barge has been recaptured. Approach within 100 meters of that recaptured barge to retake it for your side.

run-and-gun task where you'll excel only if you can quickly eliminate enemy 'Mechs with outstanding accuracy.

Water also plays an important role. Your 'Mech's top speed will be hindered by fighting with its ankles submerged. Heat sinks will operate much more efficiently, however, nicely solving the overheating problem of the past few missions (see Figure

Figure 8.5

Wading in the river does a lot for heat management issues.

8.5). That's a good thing because time is critical and you can't afford to waste precious seconds shutting down and restarting your 'Mech.

You can capture the barges by simply approaching to within 100 meters. The enemy escort won't make that an easy task, however. If you accelerate past opposing 'Mechs and head straight to the barges, you'll come under heavy fire. Balance a headstrong charge to the barges against pausing just long enough to eliminate patrol boats and Peregrines, as well as to take shots on the enemy 'Mechs.

Adjust your 'Mech's heading to face the barges and the escort. Accelerate to top speed and cycle through the nearest available enemy targets until you've pinpointed the location of any escort craft. Approach this group, which should include patrol boats, and attack using long-range Large Lasers or other laser-based weaponry. Don't take the shot if you think the discharge might strike or destroy a barge. Be patient and be accurate.

When an enemy 'Mech appears on radar (a nearby Argus should power up

TIP

Although the water increases the efficiency of heat sinks, it also slows your 'Mech considerably. There are a few areas on the side of the river where the land juts out forming a small strip to walk over. Your BattleMech will be much faster in these areas. If you're falling behind the escorts, use the land to make up some valuable time and distance.

after your assault on the patrol boats), order your lancemates to keep it occupied while you continue the charge toward the munitions barges. Peregrine combat helicopters, while weak, could pose a minor hassle. Don't stop moving; adjust your viewpoint while maintaining course and shoot the choppers down with laser weaponry.

Capturing the barges is priority one. Blast away at defending 'Mechs if you wish, but you won't complete the mission successfully if four barges aren't captured. If you're adept at dealing with multiple enemies at once, it's to your advantage to move as fast as possible through the water and reach the barges quickly.

Patrol boats and Peregrines will soon approach and pass by your 'Mech. Don't feel the need to stop and contend with the enemy units. Order lancemates to take on any enemy units you're forced to ignore. All will return and attack on second or third passes. Enemy 'Mechs will be the biggest hindrance to reaching the barges and the toughest opponent slowing you down (see Figure 8.6). Eliminate them quickly by firing an alpha strike or two as you enter combat. Keep your lancemates occupied with an enemy 'Mech while you continue toward the barges. As you near the ships, an enemy Uziel and an Argus will head you off.

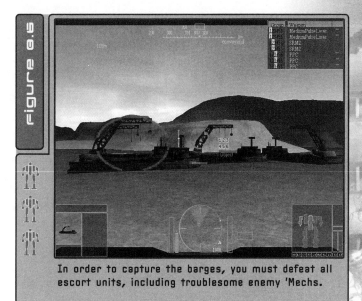

Figure 8.5

In order to capture the barges, you must defeat all escort units, including troublesome enemy 'Mechs.

The last enemy 'Mech, a Loki, follows the barges closely. By that time, you should be close enough to begin capturing the enemy vessels. Look at your radar and take note of when the blip designating each enemy barge turns from red to blue (indicating capture). The remaining enemies can be cleared from the mission area once four barges have been captured. Take care not to fire on the barges, or you could destroy your new precious cargo.

Should you hear warnings that the barges are reaching the NAV Beta destination, go into overdrive. Ignore the remaining enemy 'Mechs and do whatever it takes to reach the barges as quickly as possible. The mission ends in success once four barges are captured and the enemy escort has been eliminated.

Advancing slowly and fighting each enemy threat could prove disastrous—the barges move quickly, and it won't take the ships long to reach their NAV Beta escape point. Rush to the enemy barges. Skip the water path and take a route up one of the pieces of land that flanks the waterway. Remain on dry land for the majority of your advance. As you near the barges, return to the water and approach each in turn until four are captured. Then retreat to your lancemates and order them to engage your 'Mech pursuers.

In addition, capturing all six barges provides additional salvage bounty for the mission. In order to reach all six, you must work even faster and adeptly balance the charge to each barge with the offense and defense to survive fire from defending 'Mechs and patrol boats. Once you've captured four barges, order lancemates against nearby 'Mechs and attempt to reach the final two. You can recapture any lost barges on the way back to your lance and the enemy 'Mechs.

Operation 4, Mission 4: Destroy Factory

Mission Briefing: The destruction of a key munitions factory may cripple Steiner operations all over Kentares IV. We will try to strike at and destroy this factory with the help of a local guide in a Swiftwind. Visibility is poor, so short-range weapons may be preferable.

MechLab

Battle after battle with vehicles and tough 'Mechs (including a Nova Cat and an Awesome) characterizes this mission, where you're ordered to eliminate three enemy factories located in a fog-filled urban environment. Because of the fog, long-range weapons are nearly useless. Close-range combat superiority is key, and you must select and outfit your 'Mech accordingly.

Choose the Loki if one was salvaged from the previous mission. Close-range combat is the Loki's specialty. If the Loki is unavailable, the Thanatos or Uziel offers the next best balance of durability and firepower. Place the three lancemates in durable 'Mechs equipped for close-range combat.

Battle Plan

Objectives: Link up with your local guide. Destroy the first munitions plant.

You begin the mission on the outskirts of a city, the densest urban environment explored thus far. The opening cutscene reveals the design, color, and makeup of the factories you've been ordered to locate and destroy. One of the biggest issues you'll face during the mission is the fog—it's really thick and will create significant visibility problems as you approach enemy 'Mechs. Long-range weapons are basically useless in this pea soup mist. So be prepared for some tough close-quarters encounters.

No longer will you be able to get off an alpha strike from long range. By the time you gain sight on the enemy 'Mech, all weapons will be within range and it's kill or be killed. To counter the fog's effects, use the urban structures to your advantage. If you're near an opposing 'Mech, duck behind a nearby building and follow the target box with your 'Mech's head-up display (HUD) indicators. After the enemy BattleMech exposes itself, fire all weapons (if your 'Mech's heat levels can take the abuse) and return to your safe spot.

You'll still be able to pick up enemy 'Mechs and vehicles on radar, but they will have trouble lining you up in their crosshairs.

Urban structures can also pose problems. Scattered fuel pods and fuel trucks can be a serious hazard, and so can the buildings themselves (see Figure 8.7). Don't hesitate to fire on structures, however, as you aren't here to defend anything. Try to

Explosive fuel trucks and pods are useful in damaging enemy 'Mechs, but can pack quite a punch if stepped on inadvertently.

avoid bumping into buildings repeatedly until they explode. The resulting explosion can damage your 'Mech and increase heat levels drastically. If you're currently in battle with an enemy, the damage and the overheating could leave you vulnerable to attack. Fuel pods can be even worse. Watch your step around these volatile objects, though be sure to shoot them from a distance to damage nearby enemy 'Mechs and vehicles.

Proceed toward NAV Delta to rendezvous with Shepard in the Swiftwind. This local guide will lead the way through the dense city to each of the three munitions plants on your search and destroy list. Enemy tanks (Vedettes and Bulldogs) may hinder your advance toward the rendezvous point. Eliminate the enemy vehicles with lasers, using your lancemates to assist if needed. As you approach NAV Delta, Shepard contacts you and begins moving toward the first munitions plant.

You'll encounter significant resistance on the way to this factory. Order all lancemates to attack the powered-up enemy Shadow Cat that first appears on radar. Meanwhile, clear out the Bulldog tanks around the munitions plant. When Shepard arrives, NAV Alpha (the location of the first munitions plant) appears on your HUD. If you've wandered off attacking enemy vehicles and 'Mechs, return to NAV Alpha to level the plant. Destroy the tanks and the two Shadow Cat 'Mech guards (keep your lancemates occupied and in combat), then turn your attention to the munitions plant. Conserve ammunition here by using laser weaponry to demolish the factory.

> **TIP**
>
> Move slowly through the urban landscape. If you advance too quickly, you could trigger several enemies and come under aggressive attack from multiple hostiles. When you spot an enemy on radar, intercept it at medium speed and destroy it before moving on.

Mid-Mission Objective: Destroy the second munitions plant.

With the first munitions plant destroyed, Shepard starts down the road to the second. Follow the Swiftwind closely and order your lancemates to assume formation. As you near the second plant, an enemy Hellspawn and Nova Cat appear on radar. Shepard will notify you once she has reached the second factory, and NAV Beta will appear on your HUD indicating its location.

Keep an eye out for fuel pods here. Maneuver around the dangerous devices and attempt to lure enemy 'Mechs near. If you have trouble avoiding the pods, destroy them from a distance. Even though you won't gain the explosive benefit against your foes, you also won't have to worry about overheating or damaging your own BattleMech.

Order all three lancemates against the Nova Cat (the tougher of the two defenders) while you destroy the Hellspawn as quickly as possible. If you notice your lancemates struggling against the Nova Cat, pull them off this target and order them against the weaker Hellspawn. Of course, you can cripple the Hellspawn and order your lancemates against it while you switch to the stronger Nova Cat. When the coast is clear, finish off the munitions plant (again using laser weaponry) at NAV Beta.

Mid-Mission Objective: Destroy the third munitions plant.

With the second munitions plant destroyed, Shepard begins movement toward the final target. Order your lancemates to assume formation so they're close when you arrive; the third plant isn't very far from the second. Shepard remains well back from the last munitions plant and notifies you of its location. Her arrival triggers NAV Gamma on your HUD. Use it as a reference point to locate the factory.

The toughest battle lies here. Prepare for a duel against an enemy Awesome, a powerful BattleMech with PPC weaponry (see Figure 8.8). Multiple blasts from the PPC can rip limbs off in no time.

> **TIP**
>
> If you lose track of Shepard in the dense fog, simply cycle through friendly units (defaults to the "W" key) to pinpoint her location—if she's within radar range. If she's out of radar range, search the city until you uncover a new blue blip on radar. Cycle friendly targets again at this point to find her location.

Figure 8.8

Heavy fog forces you to combat 'Mechs at close range.

Though you're forced to assault the Awesome at close range because of the fog conditions, be sure to use neighboring structures as cover. Do whatever you can to evade that PPC blast. Keep to the side or behind the Awesome to stay out of its line of fire. While you tackle the Awesome, order your lancemates to battle the second enemy 'Mech guard, a Hellspawn (or coordinate combat vice versa, with lancemates up against the Awesome). The mission ends successfully as soon as the third munitions plant crumbles to the ground.

alternate solution

Rendezvousing with Shepard is a secondary objective and not vital to mission success. You can choose to ignore her guidance and search the city for the munitions plants yourself. Because the urban landscape is so vast, there are many ways to complete this mission. You can head to the factories in any order, though none of the NAV points that designate them will be triggered in your HUD unless you use Shepard.

Operation 4, Mission 5: Capture Prisoner Convoy

Mission Briefing: A group of your father's veteran MechWarriors are being moved to a prisoner camp for possible execution. We have helicopter assets standing by for a rescue attempt. We will strike at the convoy, destroy its escorts, then move the convoy to a landing zone (LZ) for extraction.

MechLab

Although enemy 'Mech numbers are significant here, you faced tougher individual 'Mechs in the previous mission. A 'Mech-to-'Mech battle against an Uziel occurs as the mission opens; you're ordered to destroy this 'Mech as well as the radar and control tower the enemy is defending. Overtaking the convoy escort and capturing the convoy itself accomplishes half of the remaining task. You must then defend the capturing vehicles and friendly helicopters from an aggressive enemy assault.

The Nova Cat, Loki, and Awesome (if salvaged from previous missions) are excellent choices. Each possesses enough firepower to rip through the lighter enemy

'Mech defenders and attackers. If these are unavailable, select the Vulture, Thanatos, or Uziel, depending on personal preference. Complement your 'Mech choice by placing lancemates in long-range 'Mechs (if your selection excels in close-range combat) or close-range 'Mechs (if your ride is best at long-range combat). Once again, you're in the desert. Watch your heat closely and load up on additional heat sinks if you select a primarily laser-based 'Mech.

Battle Plan

Objective: Destroy all defense radar and towers at NAV Zeta.

The deserts and foggy urban landscape of the campaign's previous missions have made way for farmland. This tranquil, portrait-worthy terrain is deceptive, though; your mission among the wooden barns and lush crops here is dangerous and extremely vital to the resistance cause (see Figure 8.9). You must capture an enemy convoy and defend it against aggressive counterattack. Prep your 'Mech for movement and battle. Organize your weapon groupings and cycle through navigation points until you reach NAV Zeta. Before you intercept the convoy, you must take out the radar and turret control tower (to disable the antiair towers).

Capture the enemy convoy and defend it against a counterattack!

An enemy Uziel 'Mech guards the radar and turret control tower at Nav Zeta. Locate the Uziel among the nearby structures and order your lancemates to attack it. While your allies engage the 'Mech in battle, target the radar dish and tower. Both should fall to a few blasts from your lasers. The destruction of the radar and tower triggers the next mission objective. Finish off the enemy Uziel before moving on to NAV Alpha. Ignore the Calliope turrets here. They're inactive against ground-based targets. Simply destroy the radar, tower, and Uziel; then proceed to NAV Alpha.

Mid-Mission Objectives: Destroy convoy escort. Destroy targets of opportunity.

The enemy convoy lies at NAV point Alpha. Adjust your heading and accelerate to full speed. Order your lancemates to assume formation. As you near the convoy, enemy Bulldogs and two Cougar 'Mechs appear on radar. Beware of a line of enemy fuel trucks entering from a side road. Don't fire on them if they near the convoy, as the explosive blast could damage or destroy a unit.

You shouldn't have trouble with the vehicles. Standard tanks and carriers should fall quickly to laser fire or simply by smashing into them. The Cougars provide a tougher challenge than the vehicles, but shouldn't pose much of a threat against you and your lancemates. Order your allies to battle one Cougar while you handle the other.

WARNING

Convoy vehicle armor is weak, making the units extremely vulnerable to attack. Stick close and intercept any incoming assailants. Use alpha strike shots at long range to weaken or cripple approaching enemy 'Mechs. Target Bulldog tanks carefully, as these enemy vehicles closely resemble convoy units from a distance. Be careful before discharging those Large Lasers!

After the escort has been disabled, the convoy is taken under your control and starts advancing toward the landing zone at NAV point Delta.

Mid-Mission Objective: Escort convoy to landing zone at NAV Delta.

An enemy Vulture 'Mech powers up near the convoy as the now-friendly units begin their advance to NAV Delta. Don't become distracted by the Vulture. Order one or two lancemates to engage it while you remain with the convoy (see Figure 8.10). If the Vulture persists in moving toward the convoy, intercept it—but don't fall too far behind (especially if you're in a slow 'Mech) as another battle waits at the landing zone.

Stick close to or preferably ahead of the convoy as you approach NAV Delta. Once at the NAV point, two enemy Uziels appear on radar. Fire upon both enemy targets right away to divert their attention away from the convoy, then order nearby lancemates against one Uziel while you contend with the second. The mission ends in success once the helicopters escape the mission area with prisoners onboard.

figure 6.10

The convoy switches affiliation as soon as the escort vehicles and 'Mechs are destroyed.

alternate solution

The mission ends if no enemies are present after the choppers lift off. A lance of enemy 'Mechs is inbound to the landing zone. It's best not to fight them. Evade them and only engage if you cannot shake them. If you keep lancemates engaged with enemy 'Mech targets, realize you may lose them to these enemy forces. Move ahead of the captured convoy and clear the landing zone before the convoy arrives. To keep their 'Mechs intact, order lancemates off of their current target (by either ordering them to your NAV point or to assume formation).

Operation 4, Mission 6: Liberate Prisoner Camp

Mission Briefing: We have gotten reliable information regarding the location of the Steiner prisoner camp. Resistance will be strong, but we need to strike at this camp and liberate the prisoners. Be prepared for fierce fighting involving the largest 'Mechs you have seen to this point.

MechLab

This is perhaps the most hectic mission you've faced thus far. You've been ordered to assault an enemy base to capture four prisoner barracks, and the base is heavily defended by stationary turrets, vehicles, and 'Mechs. An encounter with enemy MechWarrior James Kulin (in a powerful Mad Cat) and his elite escort concludes this trying assignment. 'Mech durability is key here. You must be able to survive turret and vehicle blasts as well as tough fights against defending 'Mechs. Thankfully, your lancemates as well as two additional allied 'Mechs accompany you in the base assault.

The Loki, Thanatos, Awesome, and Nova Cat are all solid choices (if available). The Awesome and its devastating PPC weaponry should prove the most effective offensively, though remember that this same PPC weaponry drives heat levels up dramatically in this desert terrain. Keep that in mind during the 'Mech selection process. You may wish to sacrifice some offensive power for additional heat sinks.

Battle Plan

Objectives: Link up with allied units. Destroy all guard towers around each of the four prisoner compounds. Destroy all 'Mechs guarding the base.

This is arguably the toughest battle you've faced thus far. In order to complete the task ahead, you must battle your way through loads of enemy defenses and climb up a well-protected hillside just to reach the enemy base...which contains even more defenses. The mission includes battles against vehicles, long-range turrets, and an assortment of medium and heavy enemy 'Mechs. It's a long struggle that requires the patience to fire with accuracy and conserve ammunition for the final confrontations inside the enemy stronghold.

Listen to the radio transmissions as the mission begins. An important rendezvous point lies at NAV Delta where you'll meet up with allied 'Mechs. Adjust your heading to this NAV point and accelerate your 'Mech to full speed. Prepare your weapon groupings as you see fit. The first targets you will face arrive from the northwest and include air units (Peregrine combat helicopters), stationary turrets, and two enemy Cougars. Order your lancemates against the 'Mechs while you clear out the turrets and choppers (see Figure 8.11).

Use laser-based weaponry, specifically long-range Large Lasers, to reduce the enemy turrets to rubble. Steer your 'Mech to the left and right as you approach to avoid taking damage from turret blasts.

Figure 6.11

Be prepared to face enemy 'Mechs early in the mission.

Continue to battle the remaining enemy forces as you make your way to NAV Delta to rendezvous with allied reinforcements. While the desert landscape is mostly barren, attempt to retreat slightly behind hills in order to get strikes on an enemy 'Mech's head, chest, shoulder, or arm armor in hopes of knocking out a weapon or destroying a limb.

When you reach NAV Delta, you'll hook up with a squad of allied reinforcements that consists of two Uziels. Listen to the radio chatter and set your navigation sights on NAV Alpha, the position of the enemy base and the prisoner barracks you're aiming to liberate. You're told at the ren-

WARNING

Let the allied reinforcements and your lancemates take punishment for you and dish out some as well. Conserve your ballistic and missile-based weaponry for the closing battles at the enemy base. Use lasers against the prisoner barracks guard towers and vehicles. The final showdown will be much easier if your 'Mech still possesses its most powerful weapons.

dezvous point that the attack can commence from the front, which contains heavy defenses, or around back, where there could be lighter support.

This suggestion is spot on. If you attack from the front, up a tough hill, you'll face additional turrets during the approach. Should you choose to move around to the base's rear, you won't face nearly as many turrets, though you'll still need to deal with some that lie within range of your position inside the enemy base. Taking the time to move around back is recommended, though you'll still battle the same number of enemy 'Mechs.

If you attempt a frontal assault, concentrate on eliminating the laser guard towers with long-range weaponry. Simultaneously battle the enemy 'Mechs, which include Catapults and Vultures, emerging from the base to intercept your assault (see Figure 8.12). The turrets aren't easy to pick off. The rocky landscape means you won't always have the best line of fire against any given tower at any particular time. You must maneuver slightly to gain sight of each tower. Of course, enemy 'Mechs won't hesitate to target you while you're lining up

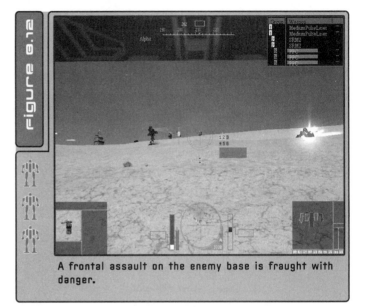

Figure 8.12

A frontal assault on the enemy base is fraught with danger.

other targets. Allow your lancemates and the reinforcements to occupy the enemy Catapults and Vultures while you eliminate as many towers as possible.

Don't simply charge into the base when the towers have been destroyed. Maintain your position and let the enemy come to you. This will make the opposing 'Mechs easy targets for the reinforcements, your lancemates, and your own BattleMech. Charging into the base will only give the advantage to your foe, and triggering the arrival of new enemy 'Mechs isn't a smart idea. As long as you have more 'Mechs (and you have plenty with the reinforcements and the lancemates), you're operating at a distinct advantage.

TIP

A turret control tower rests on a small plateau at the top of the hill adjacent to a communications station and between the two rows of enemy laser turrets. A secondary turret control tower lies on the northern edge of the base (along the mission boundary). Eliminate both towers to permanently deactivate all enemy gun emplacements.

The enemy base is crawling with Uziel 'Mechs. Keep your lancemates and allied reinforcements occupied with them, assisting whenever possible. You'll be able to utilize plenty of cover from structures and buildings if you fight the Uziels inside the enemy base. This does, however, force a tough fight against several Uziels. You might also get caught in a crossfire from guard towers, LRM Carriers, and remaining turrets. Eliminate any vehicles within range as quickly as possible and focus on opposing 'Mechs. If your lancemates' target is sufficiently crippled, order them against a fresh new enemy 'Mech.

After you've thinned the enemy 'Mech ranks, search the base for the prisoner compounds and guard towers. Destroy two guard towers around each of the four bases to complete the mission objectives. Destroying all guard towers and clearing the base of enemy 'Mech units triggers the mission's final objective.

Mid-Mission Objective: Take out James Kulin and his lancemates.

James Kulin arrives inside a Mad Cat with three Vulture lancemates. When he appears on radar, don't advance. Allow Kulin and his allies to make their way up the hill. Keep your own lancemates close by. When Kulin's Mad Cat appears over the crest of the hill, fire an alpha strike at its head or midsection. Order your mates against the Vulture 'Mechs while you tackle Kulin.

Don't hesitate to retreat into the crumbling enemy base. Use the remaining structures as cover against Kulin's attacks. Cripple his Mad Cat and cycle targets to one of the Vultures. Assist your lancemates in battle until all three 'Mechs have been destroyed. The mission ends in success once all guard towers have been taken out, the prisoners have been liberated, and Kulin's squad has been destroyed.

TIP

Search the western edge of the enemy base to uncover a Mobile Field Base. Use it to repair and rearm your BattleMech before you face James Kulin and his lancemates.

alternate solution

Assaulting the enemy base from the rear keeps you away from the row of turrets protecting the hill route. After rendezvousing with allied units, stay on the northern edge of the mission boundary and tackle the patrolling Vultures and Catapults there. Continue along the edge until you pass the base and NAV Alpha on your left. Then adjust your heading and approach the base from its less-defended backside. A rear assault also provides better line of sight against the two turret control towers, which can be eliminated to permanently deactivate all laser turrets. Knock out the control towers as soon as possible, then retreat out of the base and allow enemy 'Mechs to approach you, your lancemates, and the allied reinforcements.

operation 5: "The Greater Good" missions

The environmental effects within the fifth campaign operation, "The Greater Good," return to those of earlier missions. The dry heat of the desert has given way to wet swamplands. You'll find heat sinks working somewhat more efficiently, at least while in the water, but you now face minor speed and visibility problems. There's also not much cover in the swamp. Spare trees and occasional changes in ground level provide only limited defense against plentiful enemies.

This chapter includes complete walkthroughs for the three missions that comprise the "Greater Good" operation. You should now be adept at coordinating lancemates, equipping your weapons, armor, and equipment, and fighting enemy vehicles, base defenses, and 'Mechs. These expeditions in the swamp require superb close- and long-range combat skills. Here you will search for and destroy an enemy airfield, defend a seaside town from attack, and take on an elite enemy 'Mech in a challenging one-on-one battle.

Operation 5, Mission 1: Destroy Bombers

Mission Briefing: Steiner air assets based in a hidden base somewhere in the swampland to the south of Vale may be used as a weapon of terrorism. We cannot let them threaten the local populace any longer. Destroy the bombers and the control tower to end this threat to all noncombatants in the area.

MechLab

This mission features two significant segments. The first part consists of searching for and finally locating the enemy airfield. Along the way you will encounter Peregrine combat helicopters, stationary turrets, hovercraft, and an occasional patrolling BattleMech. The real fight begins inside the airfield, though. There you'll encounter the greatest opposition, with Shilone bombers, stationary turrets, and tough 'Mech defenders hitting you in waves.

Don't hesitate to load up with laser-based weaponry. The swamp offers a much more heat-friendly environment than the previous operation's desert landscape. Long-range weapons will serve you well during the mission's first segment, but their close-range cousins become much more important as you engage the airfield's defenders. Enemy 'Mechs are the toughest component of the mission. Pilot a durable, powerful heavy 'Mech (such as an Awesome, Nova Cat, or Thanatos) and place lance-mates inside similar ones to support your efforts.

Battle Plan

Objective: Search for the enemy airfield.

The fifth operation begins in a swamp. You're dropped down and ordered to search for an airfield located somewhere in the immediate area. Orders are to locate enemy Shilone bombers at the nearby airfield and destroy them. Knocking out the aircraft could prevent future air strikes against important allied structures. Expect to encounter enemy patrols around the swamp.

Accelerate your 'Mech and begin moving forward from your start position. Within moments, an enemy patrol (likely consisting of either a Harasser or Condor) will appear on your radar. Organize your weapon groupings. You'll face many enemy vehicles and Peregrine air units during your search for the airfield. Group laser-based weaponry together so you aren't wasting valuable ballistic or missile ammunition on relatively harmless vehicle targets. As you move to intercept the first enemy that shows up on your scope, others may appear. Expect to be overwhelmed rather quickly. The majority of opposition targets will be vehicles and air units, with the occasional missile or laser turret making its presence known as well. Be cautious and eliminate the nearest target, or any enemies targeting you, before moving on to the next. Order lancemates against specific targets (especially a patrolling 'Mech or two) as you quickly work through softer targets, such as the turrets and vehicles.

The swamp provides a change from the desert air of the previous operation. The marsh and wetland environment will slow down your 'Mech but offers a moderate improvement to heat sink efficiency. Additionally, the dense trees, murky fog, and sudden changes in elevation will create minor visibility problems. Occasionally you won't have line of fire on an enemy vehicle, 'Mech, or turret until you're right on top of it. Make use of your 'Mech's zoom to examine long-range targets closely (see Figure 9.1). Use the zoom feature to check out potential targets as well as enemy structures that might lead to the hidden airfield.

Figure 9.1

Switch on your 'Mech's visual zoom to locate long-range targets and potentially improve Large Laser accuracy.

Harassers, Peregrines, and turrets shouldn't offer much resistance. Step on enemy vehicles, although try to limit damage to your 'Mech as you will face tough battles upon entering the airfield. If you're attacked by Peregrines, back away from any vehicle targets and concentrate on eliminating the air units quickly. A few turrets are also present in the swamp. Destroy the patrols as you make your way to the airfield. Any vehicles left intact now may have to be dealt with when you uncover the Shilone bombers.

Enemy BattleMechs, patrolling the outskirts of the airfield, provide the

TIP

Treat the turrets like enemy vehicles and eliminate them from long range. If you can't get line of sight on a turret, move parallel (without getting closer) and activate your zoom until it comes into view. Then blast away with laser-based weaponry. Save ballistic and missile ammunition for enemy 'Mech targets.

greatest danger during your search. Discovering these 'Mechs (likely Shadow Cats) indicates your close proximity to the base. Lure them away from the airfield to take them on. You won't have many structures or large hills (such as those in the alpine or desert environments) for use as cover, but pulling away from the airfield should keep you from becoming overwhelmed by additional defenders, which will include other 'Mechs and launched bombers.

If you're having trouble locating the airfield, move toward the greatest congestion of enemy units (indicated by the red blips on your radar). Eliminate any patrols you encounter on the way and head toward the structures. Use your zoom to examine the hangars, control towers, and other small buildings. Clear out any outlying defenses. Blow apart these units before moving into the base against the Shilone bombers. Once inside you'll be preoccupied with destroying the aircraft and won't be able to divert your attention to any remaining defenses. Moving into the airfield triggers the next stage of the mission.

Mid-Mission Objectives: Destroy all of the Shilone bombers. Destroy the command tower. Destroy the heavy 'Mechs defending the base.

After you're inside the base, you receive a radio transmission that the enemy bombers are scrambling for takeoff (see Figure 9.2). After they reach the air, they'll circle around the airfield dropping explosive payloads on your 'Mech and lance-mates. The bombers can inflict significant damage, especially if you're preoccupied fighting other 'Mechs or base defenses. Triggering the launch of the bombers also triggers the arrival of nearby enemy defenses. Be prepared to face off against several tough heavy 'Mechs, including a Thor, Vulture, and Nova Cat. Order your lancemates against the defending

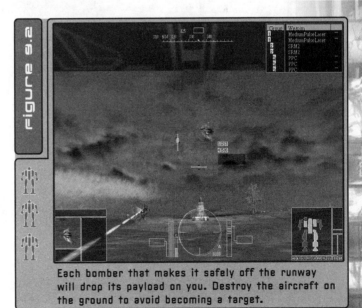

Each bomber that makes it safely off the runway will drop its payload on you. Destroy the aircraft on the ground to avoid becoming a target.

'Mechs while you target the Shilone bombers, both those still on the runway and those already in the air.

Ignore other defenses upon receiving the transmission. Accelerate your 'Mech to top speed and locate the bombers. Maneuver quickly to the first bomber you find on the ground and take shots at defenders as you move. Don't stop moving toward the bombers. You need to knock out as many as possible before they take off, as Shilone bombers are much more difficult to eliminate once airborne. They're much faster than Peregrines, and enemy 'Mechs will have arrived by this point and also be demanding your attention.

Use airfield structures for cover. Flee from enemy 'Mechs and use any opportunities to target the remaining grounded bombers. Cycle through targets frequently to locate airborne Shilones. You'll be notified when all bombers have been destroyed.

Tackle any remaining enemy 'Mechs next. Choose targets based on threat potential. If your lancemates have managed to cripple an enemy 'Mech, consider targeting another.

Shift your attention to the air control tower as soon as enemy defenses are down. It's a weak building and won't be able to withstand much punishment. The mission concludes successfully once all bombers are eliminated, the control tower has been leveled, and the airfield cleared of enemy units.

alternate solution

You have several options upon reaching the airfield. You'll likely spot the air control tower first; consider destroying it on sight rather than leaving it for later. Also, instead of concentrating on airborne Shilone bombers, order a lancemate against specific bombers as you and remaining lancemates tackle defending 'Mechs. Shilone bombers drop potentially damaging bombs, though it's the airfield's heavy 'Mech defense that poses the greatest danger. You may wish to handle the greatest danger yourself while using lancemates to clean up remaining vehicles and bombers.

Operation 5, Mission 2: Destroy Patrols

Mission Briefing: We need to split up to cover all threats to the civilian populace. Your job will be to sweep through the swamp and eliminate all enemy patrols. You can expect mostly hovercraft but do not underestimate Steiner.

MechLab

Traversing through the swamp while destroying tanks and hovercraft shouldn't be difficult considering your victories thus far. Any of the available 'Mechs should be able to survive encounters with vehicles. It's the elite Thor 'Mech discovered at mission's end that is the greatest danger. This Thor excels at long- and close-range attacks, so it's going to take consistent targeting and quick reflexes to take him out. Lieutenant Burke has mounted dual ER PPCs and won't hesitate to rip apart your armor with alpha strikes and generous helpings from his LBX Autocannon.

Prepare for the Thor, not the hovercraft. Keep your 'Mech in good condition (and equipped with plenty of missile or ballistic ammunition) to survive the final encounter. Select the heaviest available 'Mech based on personal preference. If you favor powerful PPC attacks, pilot the Awesome or Nova Cat if available. Should you prefer ballistic or missile weaponry, consider the Loki, Thanatos, or Mad Cat.

Battle Plan

Objectives: Destroy hovercraft patrols at NAVs Alpha, Beta, Gamma, and Delta.

Mission orders are fairly direct: sweep the navigation points for enemy patrols. According to the transmission, there are four groups of patrols consisting of primarily hovercraft-based vehicles. You're in the swamp once again and it's much foggier this time. Visibility is quite poor, though your radar is functioning normally. The NAV pattern for the suspected patrols has been punched into your onboard 'Mech computer. Cycle through to the closest NAV point and adjust your heading to an intercept course.

Much like the previous mission, the swamp offers significant landscape changes from the dry desert. This particular map resembles the mouth of a river delta. There are lots of river branches with strips of land separating each branch. The enemy hovercraft travel along these winding rivers and occasionally move across the narrow bits of land. You'll be trudging through the water for the most part, so expect your speed to be hindered slightly. As a trade-off, heat sinks will operate slightly more efficiently.

Enemy targets (Condors and Harassers) should begin to appear on your radar as you approach the first NAV point. Cycle to the nearest opposition vehicle and approach. The strips of land that divide the river branches obscure your view and will pose problems if you hope to pick off the hovercraft at long range. There's no time crunch here, however, so feel free to wait until the hovercraft move into view before moving to close quarters. Each hovercraft on its own isn't particularly threatening, but if you approach to within their line of fire, your 'Mech could take substantial damage from the entire group (see Figure 9.3).

Try to avoid facing heavy numbers of hovercraft and snipe as many as possible from long range.

As in previous missions, don't waste your best weapons on such minor threats as the hovercraft. You won't have much trouble as long as you avoid fighting several vehicles at once. Use the raised sections of land as cover and don't hesitate to retreat behind the hills until you can lure the hovercraft into a more advantageous position.

Stick with laser-based weapons when dealing with the vehicles. Save your powerful ammunition for the tough 'Mech battle you'll encounter at the mission's conclusion. Likewise, attack the hovercraft cautiously to minimize damage to your 'Mech.

Upon finishing up at one NAV point, cycle to the next and continue the process. Clearing a NAV point triggers a transmission notifying you of partial completion and how many patrols remain. Expect the batches of hovercraft to spread during the mission.

TIP

Traversing land takes time. If you're inside a 'Mech with Jump Jet ability, launch over the strips and fire at the vehicles within range on the way down. Moving quickly across the land obstacles can also help you escape a concentrated batch of hovercraft and allow you to evaluate your attack approach.

Though they begin rather clustered together, they will maneuver through the wetlands and could attack from several angles if you aren't cautious. Remain behind cover until you gain line of sight on all nearby hovercraft.

If during the course of battle, you find yourself severely damaged or out of ballistic ammunition, take advantage of the field base in this mission. It is located near the small outpost in between NAV Alpha and NAV Beta. Due to the elite level of Lieutenant Burke and the importance of this battle, you should definitely make a trip to the Mobile Field Base before you take out the last hovercraft patrol. This will ensure you possess a fresh 'Mech for the mission's final one-on-one confrontation.

The campaign against the patrols ends once all NAV points have been searched and all hovercraft destroyed. After destruction of the second to last patrol group, you receive a transmission reporting unusual readings on radar. Finish off the final hovercraft patrol group as you did the others, and the source of the unusual readings becomes clear. Enemy MechWarrior Duncan Burke begins taunting you over radio transmission. He's somewhere in the swamp and you'll have to deal with him (see Figure 9.4)! Prepare for the battle by assessing your weapon groupings. Ready a group of long-range weapons to damage Burke as he approaches. Hold off on firing close-range weaponry until Burke's Thor closes within range.

Duncan Burke arrives in a powerful Thor 'Mech.

It's an intense fight against Burke. The Thor carries some devastating close-range weapons and the BattleMech combat veteran knows how to use them. Attempting to face Burke at close range could prove costly if you can't avoid his deadly LBX Autocannons. Take long-range shots at the Thor as you approach, then duck behind one of the strips of land and lure it into a close-up alpha strike ambush. When his Thor appears in your line of fire, adjust your crosshairs to the upper torso and fire. Monitor Burke's damage levels and pound away at his 'Mech's most vulnerable areas.

Don't hesitate to retreat from the battle if you're not faring well at close range. Repeat ambush tactics by retreating, taking cover, and luring Burke into your line of fire. Powerful ballistic or PPC weaponry provides the best method of quick destruction. Retreat to the water to keep heat levels down and pound away at Burke's damaged armor. The mission concludes with success after clearing the patrols and destroying Burke's Thor 'Mech.

Operation 5, Mission 3: Defend Exodus

Mission Briefing: The city of Vale is endangered even despite our best efforts. We have been evacuating civilians but time is short. Two civilian ships remain at the docks still taking on civilians. We need to buy these ships as much time as possible and guard them as they attempt to get out to sea.

MechLab

Heavy enemy 'Mechs populate this defensive mission—you'll need equivalent durability and firepower in order to survive. You'll also face patrol boats and some Bulldog tank squads, but neither present a threat equal to the enemy Nova Cat and Awesome 'Mechs. Optimizing the use of your lancemates is vital to mission success. Be sure to place them inside available heavy 'Mechs.

You should have a varied selection of salvaged BattleMechs by this point in the game. The battles from here onward continue to escalate in difficulty, making durability and stamina as important as sheer firepower as there is no opportunity to repair. Pilot a heavy, durable 'Mech and base its weaponry on personal preferences. Laser-based devices will still cause moderate heat problems here, so keep this in mind. Of course, ballistic and missile weaponry require ammunition. Fit your 'Mech primarily with close-range, 'Mech-to-'Mech combat equipment. Support this with a few long-range weapons for use against air units, patrol boats, and incoming enemy 'Mechs.

Battle Plan

Objectives: Protect the refugee ships until they can reach the open sea. Destroy all hostile units in the immediate area.

Evacuation ships filled with refugees are being loaded at the docks (positioned near NAV Beta) and the nearby fuel depot (located at NAV Alpha) is currently under attack from Steiner's Bulldog tanks with incoming Nightshade air units and heavy 'Mechs. Target the Bulldogs and take them out with long-range lasers. Assign targets for your lancemates and eliminate the tanks as soon as possible. You won't have time to worry about them as you take on the city's greater dangers, the Nightshades and incoming 'Mechs.

The Nightshades arrive first and bombard the city structures (and your lance) with air-to-surface missiles. Nightshades are much quicker than Peregrine combat helicopters and don't offer an easy target by hovering in place for your lasers. Accelerate quickly toward the town and target each aircraft in turn (see Figure 9.5). Order lancemates against the Nightshades as well. Send a lancemate to intercept any enemy 'Mechs that show up at this point. Ground as many Nightshades as possible before you're diverted by the arriving 'Mechs.

Incoming enemy 'Mechs include the powerful Nova Cat and

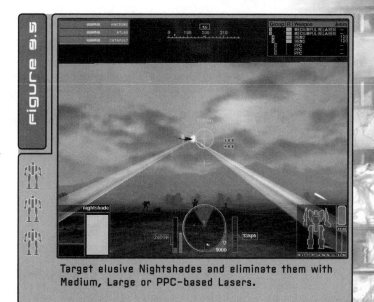

Target elusive Nightshades and eliminate them with Medium, Large or PPC-based Lasers.

Awesome. Order all lancemates against one enemy 'Mech while you eliminate the remaining Nightshades. If you come under attack from one of the BattleMechs, divert your fire to the nearby 'Mech. Monitor Nightshade locations using your radar (and by cycling through targets) and attempt to finish the air units off while simultaneously battling the enemy 'Mech. The Nova Cat and Awesome are especially tough heavy 'Mechs. Take leg shots to cripple and destroy these powerful opponents.

There's not much cover available around the outskirts of the city. If absolutely necessary, you could lure an enemy 'Mech to the water outside town and battle it there. Heat sinks work moderately better in water, and the nearby hills can be used to stage hit-and-run attacks against a pursuing 'foe. Keeping the battle inside the town also has its advantages. Look for opportunities to lure enemy 'Mechs near the fuel tanks. Fire upon the fuel tanks with an adjacent enemy 'Mech to cause damage and instant overheating.

> **TIP**
>
> More enemy 'Mechs (a second Nova Cat and a second Awesome) arrive moments after the first, so don't waste time eliminating the initial squad. Conserve as much ammunition as possible for use against the later arrivals, though you should only need laser-based weaponry to destroy the mission's final set of enemy encounters, the patrol boats and destroyers.

As you battle the 'Mech(s), make your way toward NAV Beta and the city docks. At some point during city defense, enemy patrol boats will approach the docks. Cycle to NAV Beta and head out to sea.

The patrol boats aren't especially tough but arrive in large numbers. Sink them with long-range lasers (or missiles, if available) and continue the fight against any remaining enemy 'Mechs. Make sure your lancemates join the battle against the patrol boats if they're finished against the 'Mech force. Not long after the first wave of ships arrives, the enemy sends in two destroyers, the *Thunderchild* and *Indomitable*, with long-range weaponry to fire upon the refugee boats (see Figure 9.6).

Figure 9.6

Intercept the destroyers as they arrive. Pummel them from long range and keep them away from the refugee ships.

Proceed farther out to sea and annihilate the destroyers with lasers and any remaining ballistic- or missile-based weaponry. Feel free to let them have it with everything you've got, as they're your final targets.

Mid-Mission Objective: Escort refugee boats to the open sea (NAV Delta).

At some point, the refugee boats begin moving out to sea and NAV Delta. Cycle to this NAV point, target the friendly ships, and order lancemates to guard your current target or to attack any remaining enemy targets. Assume position next to the refugee boats until you reach NAV Delta. Evacuating the boats to NAV Delta triggers mission success and the end of the operation.

alternate solution

The refugee ships load and move out after a certain amount of time. Failing to destroy present enemy forces (patrol boats and the destroyers specifically) could put the refugee ships in danger as they move out to the open sea and NAV point Delta. Though it's possible to complete the mission without aggressively engaging the patrol boats and destroyers, it's very difficult to keep the refugee ships protected from a heavy amount of enemy fire. Order your lancemates to assist your efforts in the sea and to attack specific patrol boat and destroyer targets. Escorting the refugee ships to the open sea is a breeze if all or most enemy sea targets are destroyed.

operation 6: "The Darkest Hour" missions

A forbidding, dense urban world sets the stage for MechWarrior 4's sixth operation, "The Darkest Hour." Though environmental effects are minimal (except for the dark sky and light rain), the tall skyscrapers all around provide a unique battle arena for the giant, lumbering BattleMechs. In order to survive these missions, you must be adept at using urban structures for cover and skilled at guiding your lancemates in attacks against multiple heavy targets.

This chapter includes complete walkthroughs for the five missions that make up "The Darkest Hour" operation. Powerful, heavy enemy 'Mechs populate the urban landscape and present extremely difficult targets for you and your lancemates. Study the surroundings well and be prepared to duck behind skyscrapers and into alleyways to avoid coming under fire from multiple opponents.

Operation 6, Mission 1: Reconnaissance in Force

Mission Briefing: We are entering a thick urban environment to deal the final blow to Steiner. We need to scout and destroy any Steiner units that we uncover. Urban fighting is often close-range and brutal; staying aware of your surroundings will increase the chance of survival.

MechLab

Like other reconnaissance missions, this first foray into an urban environment quickly turns into a BattleMech trial of survival. Many enemy targets will be encountered along the way, including stationary turrets, vehicles, and powerful heavy 'Mechs. In order to complete the mission, you must minimize damage, conserve ammunition, and optimize lancemate usage.

Five operations have stocked your 'Mech salvage with an assortment of light, medium, and heavy BattleMechs. Powerful close-range weaponry is a must here. Effective long-range firepower provides occasional usefulness against incoming enemies, but the tall, dense skyscrapers force most battles to close quarters. Pilot a close-range specialist, such as the Thanatos, Awesome, Loki, or Daishi (if available). Outfit lancemates in other available heavy 'Mechs (unless you're afraid to lose them) and adjust their weaponry to emphasize close-range combat.

Battle Plan

Objectives: Destroy all enemy units at NAV points Alpha, Beta, Gamma, Delta, and Epsilon.

The resistance wishes to set up a base in this sector, so the region must be cleared of enemy units in order to proceed. You're ordered on a reconnaissance patrol of five separate navigation points. As with many other recon missions, this routine task will quickly turn into a deadly battle.

You will encounter many tough 'Mechs during this patrol, as well as other assorted vehicles and stationary turrets. In order to complete the mission, you must be patient and allow your lancemates to assist your efforts. Conserving ammunition and keeping your 'Mech intact are vital to surviving the plentiful dangers encountered at each navigation point. Begin by cycling through NAV points until you locate NAV Alpha. Accelerate your 'Mech to proceed. Order your lancemates to form up or to go to your selected NAV point.

The urban landscape provides unique terrain for the coming battles. There are many opportunities to take cover against enemy 'Mech, turret, and vehicle fire. If you're struggling, look for a nearby alley or street and get behind a structure as soon as possible. Keeping the building between you and the target, allow the enemy 'Mech or vehicle to come to you. This will typically provide you with a quick, and rather easy, kill shot on the enemy vehicle or a devastating blast at the enemy 'Mech's leg, chest, or head area. Use the urban environment to your advantage and avoid doing open battle in the center of a broad street (see Figure 10.1).

Approach NAV Alpha cautiously and monitor your radar for the nearest enemy target. Attempt to lure these targets to you. If you rush to the NAV point, you may have to face all the enemies at once—not an easy task even for you and your lancemates. As you have four more NAV points to go, fighting unwisely right off the bat could prove costly when you're trying to survive the tougher battles to come. NAV

Figure 10.1

Avoid fighting groups of enemy 'Mechs in a wide street where foes can attack from all sides.

Alpha includes stationary turrets and a powerful Awesome enemy 'Mech. A shutdown Mad Cat also lies near the NAV point. The Mad Cat powers up approximately 30 seconds after the attack on NAV Alpha begins. Order lancemates to attack the Awesome while you search for the Mad Cat—which won't appear on radar until it powers up. Look toward the right-hand side of the intersection at NAV Alpha to locate the Mad Cat. Destroy or severely damage the Mad Cat before it can power up and return fire.

NOTE

You aren't restricted to following the NAV points in alphabetical order, so feel free to proceed however you wish. There's no real advantage to exploring the NAV points backwards or randomly, though the toughest battle awaits you at the "final" navigation point, NAV Epsilon.

Order your lancemates against the Awesome while you finish off the turrets as quickly as possible. Alternatively, locate the turret control vehicle in the center of the intersection. Shooting the turret control vehicle will disable all turrets at NAV

Alpha. Allow your lancemates to occupy the Awesome while you sneak in later and take shots at its most damaged areas. Go for the legs to slow down or cripple the Awesome, but focus your fire on the upper torso if the chest has already taken damage.

Concentrate all fire on the Awesome in hopes of taking down the tough 'Mech before others arrive. If you're targeted by it, retreat around the nearest structure and encourage it to follow. Alpha strike the Awesome when it comes into your line of fire. Repeat as necessary until the large 'Mech tumbles. Cycle through targets and shift your firepower onto any remaining 'Mechs or turrets. You'll receive a transmission once the NAV point is cleared, and the objective will also be removed from the list.

Cycle to NAV Beta and accelerate to top speed. Make sure your lancemates have joined you; either order them to resume formation or to proceed to your selected destination. NAV Beta includes Bulldog tanks, SRM Carriers, and a tough Atlas 'Mech. Assign your lancemates to the Atlas while you quickly finish off the tanks and SRM Carriers. Step on the vehicles if necessary. Do whatever you can to eliminate them quickly so you can join your lancemates against the Atlas.

As you did at the previous NAV point with the Awesome, keep all lancemates occupied with the Atlas until you can join them. When you arrive, target the Atlas' head with an alpha strike to destroy the enemy 'Mech quickly (see Figure 10.2). Monitor your lancemates' damage levels carefully. If some lancemates are taking too much fire, order them away from the Atlas and let the others finish off the enemy. Save all lancemates for future NAV points—you'll need as much firepower as you can muster.

Observe an enemy BattleMech's damage levels on your head-up display (HUD) and fire on its most damaged areas.

Explore NAV Gamma and Delta as you have Alpha and Beta. Both include additional enemy 'Mechs (expect to face an assortment of Argus, Mad Cat, and Awesome models) as well as

Bulldog tanks and turrets. The Mad Cat at NAV Gamma starts shut down like the one found at NAV Alpha. Locate this 'Mech near Gamma and weaken or destroy the Mad Cat before it can power up. You'll also find a turret control vehicle at Gamma to disable nearby stationary turrets.

Take one NAV point at a time. Don't trigger too many enemies at once, as the assault will likely be more than you and your now-damaged team can handle. Concentrate all firepower on a single enemy 'Mech to eliminate it quickly. Then cycle to the next nearest target and engage it. Go for the head and chest areas while ignoring the temptation to try finesse shots at specific body parts. Targeting arms and legs is tougher, even though it could blast off a weapon or cripple the enemy 'Mech.

NAV Epsilon is the location of the most dangerous targets. Not only are the plentiful turrets (with a turret control vehicle nearby), Bulldogs, SRM Carriers, and two Atlas 'Mechs found here very difficult to handle, but the navigation point lies just outside the city in an open field. You have no means for cover against enemy fire. A small pond lies just before the line of turrets. The water will moderately affect your BattleMech's ability to cool down, but don't expect much assistance against the two Atlas 'Mechs and accompanying turrets.

Attempt to lure the Atlas BattleMechs back to the city so you have the means to take cover. Stay away from the stationary turrets; it's unwise to approach close and come under fire from so many enemy units. Tackle the Atlas 'Mechs near the city. Order remaining lancemates against one Atlas while you bombard the other. Finish off the SRM Carriers as soon as possible. The mission concludes once all five NAV points have been cleared of enemy units.

Operation 6, Mission 2: Rescue Pilots

Mission Briefing: There are friendly 'Mech pilots stranded behind enemy lines. Proceed through the NAV points to locate their position. They will reveal their position with flares. A helicopter will proceed to your location for air evacuation.

MechLab

The search for the downed pilots and their parking garage hideout sends you through heavily populated enemy territory. You'll encounter many enemy 'Mechs during the hunt. Thankfully, all are light or medium class models and shouldn't offer a significant challenge against your heavy BattleMech. The enemy numbers are great, however. Attempt to battle a few at a time and avoid difficult combat situations where you're facing three or four enemy 'Mechs at once.

Close-range combat reigns supreme. Select your favorite heavy 'Mech—the Atlas from the previous mission, if salvaged, makes a fine choice—and equip it with mostly close-range weaponry. You may wish to outfit some long-range devices for use in firing upon incoming 'Mechs, especially once the parking garage has been found and you've been ordered to defend the rescue operation.

Battle Plan

Objectives: Find the parking garage holding the downed pilots. Defend the rescue helicopter.

The downed resistance pilots have holed themselves up in a parking garage located somewhere within the city. Command has entered navigation points into your onboard computer denoting the locations of separate parking garages where the pilots could be hiding. Once you locate your com-

NOTE

The correct parking garage is randomly chosen each time you play the mission. In one instance, the downed pilots might be found at NAV Alpha. Run through the mission again, however, and the correct parking garage might be at NAV Beta.

rades, a rescue helicopter will be sent to aid in their evacuation. You must protect the rescue helicopter from enemy counterattack.

Select NAV Alpha and order your lancemates to enter formation or to proceed toward your selected navigation point. Unlike the previous mission, enemy 'Mechs aren't crowding each particular NAV point; instead, they're scattered through the city streets on patrol. It's possible to complete the mission avoiding these encounters. As soon as you find the parking garage, however, the helicopter lands and you must defend it and the structure from these patrolling 'Mechs until the pilots are rescued. The more enemy 'Mechs still standing when you find the garage, the more you're forced to deal with when the helicopter arrives (see Figure 10.3).

Fortunately, most of the enemy patrols consist of light and medium 'Mechs. You'll face one heavy Thor, but most encounters will include Shadow Cats, Cougars, or Chimeras. These 'Mechs can be finished off rather quickly, especially if you're concentrating all fire with your lancemates. Monitor your radar and intercept lone enemy 'Mechs quickly. Avoid letting them come to you, as that might result in a battle with multiple targets. The more BattleMechs that converge on your location, the tougher time you will have emerging from the fight undamaged.

Exploit the urban environment by using the buildings as cover. Keep all lancemates focused on an enemy 'Mech. Monitor its damage status, and when it's been crippled, send your lancemates against

Don't ignore the enemy patrols. You'll eventually lure them to the downed pilots if you aren't careful.

another foe while you finish it off. Work your way to NAV Alpha and locate the first parking garage, a small gray building with multiple levels.

As you approach, command sends a radio transmission notifying you if the particular parking garage contains the downed pilots. If you receive an affirmative answer, remain there and prepare to defend the garage and helicopter (on its way) against patrolling enemy 'Mechs. If the parking garage is empty, cycle to the next navigation point/garage and adjust your heading to intercept. Instruct your lancemates to resume formation as you proceed. If enemy 'Mechs remain on your radar, move to attack them before approaching the next garage. Each enemy 'Mech is on a timer once the correct parking garage has been found. At different times, each enemy 'Mech will make a beeline for the parking garage. Destroying these nearby patrolling 'Mechs prior to discovering the correct garage is highly recommended.

You need to examine each navigation point (Alpha, Beta, Gamma, Delta, and Epsilon) until the right garage is located. The parking garage with the downed pilots could be at any of those navigation points, so keep searching until the correct structure has been uncovered. New patrolling 'Mechs could appear at any point along the way. Avoid any nearby navigation point until you have dealt with the 'Mech presence nearby.

Mid-Mission Objective: Defend the parking garage until your rescue chopper is loaded.

Command sends a transmission upon your reaching the correct navigation point and parking garage. You're ordered to defend the garage and helicopter until the downed pilots are safely away (see Figure 10.4). Target the nearest enemy (if any remain) and order your

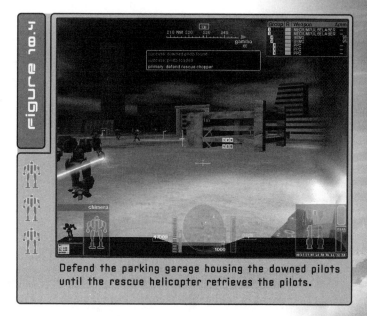

Defend the parking garage housing the downed pilots until the rescue helicopter retrieves the pilots.

lancemates to attack. You can engage that target or select another if one exists.

Successfully defending the parking garage and rescue helicopter depends greatly on the number of remaining enemy 'Mechs. If you took the time to clear out most of the patrols, you shouldn't have a difficult time keeping the parking garage safe. If you rushed through the navigation points and ignored targets of opportunity, you may face tougher opposition upon discovering the correct parking garage. The mission concludes in success once the helicopter arrives, rescues the downed pilots, and safely exits the mission area.

Operation 6, Mission 3: Destroy Base

Mission Briefing: We have located a Steiner base at the location of the local university. We may be able to get valuable intel from the base. 'Mech forces may be light, but reports state that static defenses are heavy. There is a generator that you can destroy to deprive these static weapons of power.

MechLab

Orders are to eliminate the guards around the university base. Optional orders include destruction of the turret power generator and communications center. Both decrease mission difficulty slightly and should be pursued.

Durability takes priority over speed when selecting a BattleMech. The urban environment is dense, providing plenty of cover but restricting movement. Select an available heavy 'Mech and outfit close-range weaponry to deal with the Vultures, Uziels, and Mad Cat MK. IIs found in this mission. Ballistic devices, powerful lasers, and Short-Range Missiles work well against the enemy 'Mechs in this urban environment.

Battle Plan

Objectives: Destroy all units defending the local university at NAV Alpha. Destroy the turret power generator at NAV Beta. Destroy the communications center at NAV Gamma.

Enemy forces have converted a local university into an intelligence headquarters. The university is expected to be well guarded, especially by stationary turret defenses. Orders are to destroy all the enemy units defending the former school, located at NAV Alpha. You can make the task easier by completing two optional objectives located at NAV Beta and NAV Gamma.

A turret power generator is located at NAV Beta. Destroying this station will disable all turret defenses surrounding the university, leaving only the enemy 'Mechs and vehicles to deal with at NAV Alpha. The power generator is defended by its own turrets, Bulldog tanks, and Vulture and Uziel 'Mechs (see Figure 10.5). At NAV Gamma, you'll

Figure 10.5

Take out the turret power generator to disable the enemy turrets at the university. Neglecting the objective creates a tougher battle at NAV Alpha.

find a communications center. Eliminating this base jams signal transmissions between enemy 'Mechs, which will cut off communication between enemy 'Mechs and leave them more vulnerable to your offensive. This means you can shoot one enemy 'Mech and others will not come to its aid. You will be able to pull individual units away from the university and take them out one-on-one or with the aid of lancemates. A Mad Cat MK. II defends the communications center at NAV Gamma.

Both the NAV Beta and NAV Gamma objectives are optional, but make the assault on the university much easier. Cycle through NAV points to select NAV Beta. Adjust your BattleMech's heading and proceed toward the navigation point at top speed. Order your lancemates to join formation or proceed to your selected NAV point. You'll notice an Uziel, a Vulture, Bulldogs, and turrets as you approach NAV Beta. These defenses protect the turret power generator you're trying to destroy. Order lancemates against the defending 'Mechs, while you take out the turret control towers and Bulldog tanks.

Use laser-based weaponry on the turrets and vehicles. Save your ballistic and missile weapons to use against the Vulture and Uziel here or the enemy 'Mechs you'll face at NAV Gamma and at the university. Annihilate the turret power generator once all defenses are down. Destroying the generator disables the turrets at the university (NAV Alpha). From here you can proceed immediately to the university or complete the second optional objective of destroying the communications center at NAV Gamma.

Proceed to NAV Gamma next. Order lancemates to attack the Mad Cat MK. II guarding the communications center. Knocking out the communications center jams transmissions between the enemy 'Mechs. With those down, you should face an easier battle at the university. Head to the former school at NAV Alpha after you've finished up here.

If you destroyed the turret power generator at NAV Beta, you won't have to worry about the plentiful defensive turrets that surround the university structure. There are still plenty of enemy units to battle, however. Order your lancemates to fire on the nearest enemy 'Mech while you move against the Bulldog tanks (see Figure 10.6). Destroy the vehicles as quickly as possible and join your lancemates in combat against the remaining enemy 'Mechs, which include several Chimera and Uziel 'Mechs.

There are alleys and structures all around the university plaza. Don't hesitate to back away from the fight and take on a 'Mech in the alleyways between the tall buildings. The university grounds are rather open and you could come under fire from multiple opponents. If you take the fight to the surrounding buildings, you should have enough cover to protect yourself against multiple attacks. Terminate all vehicle, turret (if applicable), and 'Mech defenders surrounding the university to complete the mission with success.

Figure 10.9

Eliminate the Bulldogs after sending your lancemates against the university's 'Mech defenders.

alternate solution

The optional objectives at NAV Beta and NAV Gamma can be completed in either order. You can also choose to skip over the optional objectives and head directly to NAV Alpha and the university. The defenses are rather light at NAV Beta and Gamma, though, so it's to your advantage to take out the turret power generator and communications center.

Operation 6, Mission 4: Rescue Sister

Mission Briefing: The unit your sister was leading has been overrun. Enter the combat area and search for her location. You must hurry; if Steiner's forces know your sister is out there, they will not hesitate to fire upon her.

MechLab

Uncovering your sister's position requires clearing Steiner's forces from the mission area. Quick, powerful combat is needed to handle the powerful heavy 'Mechs and troublesome tank squads. You must defeat enemy forces fast to prevent your sister's detection. Her position only appears as a NAV point once the mission area has been cleared.

Choose a heavy hitter from your salvage supply—the more durable the 'Mech, the better. Don't neglect firepower, though. Equip powerful close-range weaponry (an ample number of Autocannons, for instance). Watch your ammunition carefully as you proceed, as locating your sister is only the beginning. You must escort her medical evacuation unit to safety and will come under attack from additional enemy forces.

Battle Plan

Objective: Locate your sister.

You enter this urban map with no knowledge of your sister's location. Command sends a transmission that they're attempting to contact various patrols and your sister in hopes of pinpointing her location. So far, though, no one has responded to these messages. During the mission, command will continue trying to contact her. You'll be able to hear these transmissions and any responses (or lack thereof). Damon Squire accompanies you and your lancemates on the mission. He will not follow your orders but will defend your sister no matter the cost.

Meanwhile, you're ordered to sweep the map to try and uncover your sister's whereabouts. Along the way expect to encounter Bulldog tanks and an assortment of enemy 'Mechs, including Nova Cats and Awesomes. The key to this mission is clearing out some of the hostiles. Command won't receive a communication response until you take care of potential enemy threats.

You'll spot enemy units on your radar as soon as the mission begins. A group of Bulldog tanks lies approximately 900 meters from your start position. Adjust your 'Mech's heading and accelerate to top speed and investigate. Order your lancemates to maneuver into formation and assign them specific targets as you approach. Should you encounter any enemy 'Mechs (two Nova Cats are in the vicinity) near the tank group, order your lancemates to fight them while you eliminate all tanks (see Figure 10.7). When finished, join your lancemates against the enemy 'Mechs.

Don't get stuck in prolonged fights, however; remember that the enemy is also searching for your sister. The longer you take, the greater the chance that the enemy will locate her before you do, which ends the mission in failure. You must destroy enemy units quickly in order to complete the mission with success.

Eliminate all enemy units as quickly as possible. Monitor enemy 'Mech damage levels and target heavily damaged areas. Go for the legs if possible (to cripple or topple the enemy 'Mech), but if the upper torso has been battered the most, fire there in hopes of taking the enemy out quickly. Resume your patrol as soon as your foes have been destroyed or crip-

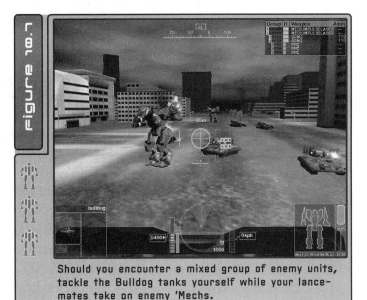

Figure 10.1

Should you encounter a mixed group of enemy units, tackle the Bulldog tanks yourself while your lancemates take on enemy 'Mechs.

pled. Order your lancemates to join you as you continue patrolling the dense city. Command will continue to radio other allied units for a position report. A radio response to that position report request means that your sister has been located.

Continue to move up and down the city streets intercepting any enemy units that you encounter. Monitor your radar closely and adjust your heading to move toward the nearest red enemy blip. Arrange your lancemates strategically and order them against specific 'Mech targets. Assist your lancemates whenever possible, though concentrate on your own enemy 'Mech target if you think you can eliminate it quickly. A similar group of Bulldogs and two Nova Cats patrols near the first. Engage these units quickly and demolish the small squad.

TIP

If your lancemates are occupied with a single enemy 'Mech, consider moving on and resuming your patrol sweep. Your lancemates should easily overwhelm a lone foe. Cripple the enemy 'Mech yourself if necessary, then continue forward.

The mission isn't complete when your scope is clear of enemy targets. Order your lancemates to assume formation and accelerate your 'Mech to top speed. Proceed in a new patrol direction and you'll soon uncover additional foes. You'll encounter a final 'Mech group containing two Awesomes as well as a small squad of Bulldog tanks. Knock out the tanks and order your lancemates against one of the 'Mechs. Join your lancemates once the Bulldogs have been destroyed. Use the nearby skyscrapers as cover against the 'Mechs.

All this time, command continues to send transmissions to the patrols in search of your sister. You won't receive a response until all enemy units are destroyed—allied units were afraid to transmit previously in fear that Steiner forces might be listening in. You're told that your sister is located inside a medical evacuation unit (essentially an ambulance) and can be found at NAV Beta. Select NAV Beta (if it already isn't aligned in your directional indicator) and put the pedal down. Follow the

NOTE

If you can locate the two surviving mobile HQs, they may be able to provide the location of your sister.

heading to the waypoint and make sure your lancemates have joined your advance. Order the lancemates to resume 'Mech formation or to proceed toward your selected NAV point.

Mid-Mission Objective: Escort your sister to NAV Zeta.

Your sister can be found in a clearing at NAV Beta (see Figure 10.8). A friendly unit (indicated by the blue radar blip) should appear on scope as you near the clearing. This is your sister's medical evacuation unit. Target the evac and prepare to escort the vulnerable vehicle to NAV Zeta.

Figure 10.8

Protect the fragile evac unit from enemy attack as you escort your sister to NAV Zeta.

Make sure that your lancemates accompany you on the escort. Keep them alongside the ambulance and order them to attack any incoming enemy units. An ambush waits at NAV Zeta. Order your lancemates to proceed ahead to the NAV point. Slow down and force the evac to halt. Four Mad Cat MK. IIs wait for your squad and the ambulance at NAV Zeta.

Order your lancemates to attack. Take your own 'Mech into weapons range and begin firing with long-range weaponry. Cripple the Mad Cats as soon as possible and escort your sister's medical evacuation unit to the NAV point at the earliest opportunity. The mission concludes in success once the vehicle carrying your sister reaches NAV point Zeta. If the ambulance is destroyed at any point, the mission ends in failure.

Operation 6, Mission 5: Capture Supplies

Mission Briefing: Steiner has a cache of weapons hidden somewhere in this city. Proceed through the NAV points to locate the cache. Beware, Steiner will be ready for you and an ambush is a possibility. A lot was sacrificed for this chance, so make it count.

MechLab

The mission's initial battle—or, in better terms, ambush—against elite Lokis and a Mad Cat MK. II is one of the toughest combat situations you'll face in the game. Effective use of lancemates is key. Additional mission targets include several long-range Calliope turrets. Consider implementing a form of long-range weaponry (either missiles or lasers) to weaken or destroy these gun emplacements from a distance.

As this is the penultimate mission, you should have a plentiful stock of heavy 'Mechs at your disposal in the MechLab. Assign each lancemate a heavy 'Mech and upgrade each to close-range weaponry, if available and possible. Pilot a heavy 'Mech of your own and make sure to take at least one long-range weapon to deal with the Calliope turrets protecting each weapons bunker. You'll find the Atlas (if salvaged) quite powerful at both close range (with its PPC and Gauss weaponry) and long range (with its LRMs). The Daishi, if available, also carries enough firepower to survive the ambush and subsequent battles against turrets and elite 'Mechs, including Castro's own custom Daishi.

Battle Plan

Objectives: Find the weapons cache and defeat Jeanine Castro. Proceed to bunkers one, two, and three and check for the cache (blow the doors off each bunker).

Orders are to bolster allied supplies and salvage (for better armaments to use in the game's final mission) by searching the city's three armory bunkers. One bunker is located at each of the three separate NAV points: NAV Alpha, NAV Beta, and NAV Gamma. Approach each bunker, blow off the doors, and search inside for the weapons cache.

The mission begins with a cutscene showing you and your lancemates walking through the city streets as you receive orders from command regarding the armory bunkers. As you watch this clip, your 'Mech wanders into the line of fire of four BattleMechs—you've been ambushed! As soon as you gain control, target the nearest enemy 'Mech and order your lancemates to attack. You're immediately under fire from all four enemies. The enemy lance targets your 'Mech exclusively!

Consider backing into the city and attempting to lure an enemy 'Mech into an ambush. Pummel any approaching enemy 'Mech with an alpha strike. Aim for the head or shatter a leg; only one mission is left in this operation, and these opponents are too tough to worry about selective targeting and salvage (see Figure 10.9).

As soon as the enemy 'Mech has been sufficiently crippled (a leg blown off or most of its weapon systems destroyed), cycle to the next enemy 'Mech and engage. The enemy lance includes three Lokis and one Mad Cat MK. II. Continue through all enemy targets until the ambushing enemy

Figure 10.9

You've been ambushed! Draw individual enemy 'Mechs away from the group and take cover behind nearby skyscrapers.

'Mechs are destroyed. You must use available structures for cover. The 'Mechs are far too powerful to handle in a toe-to-toe battle in the open street.

These 'Mechs present an extremely difficult battle at the beginning of the mission. If you're to survive the entire expedition, you must make it through this ambush suffering as little damage as possible. Don't continue on to the armory bunkers until all four 'Mechs have been eliminated.

WARNING

Don't advance against the armories until you have pin-pointed the location of the Calliope turrets surrounding the bunker. Approach each turret so you can duck behind nearby structures for cover. Peek out, fire upon the Calliope turret nearby, and then return behind the building for cover.

Approach the first bunker at NAV Alpha and clear out the defending Bulldog tanks and Calliope turrets before advancing. The Calliope turrets are very powerful and (especially if you were weakened by the ambush at the mission's start) could damage your 'Mech even further and possibly knock out a weapon system or blow off a limb. Don't underestimate their power. Once all defenses have been cleared, approach the bunker and find the front door. Blow open the door and reveal the weapons cache inside.

Cycle to the next navigation point, NAV Beta or Gamma, and approach its armory bunker (see Figure 10.10). Destroy the defenses as you did at NAV Alpha. Retreat through the alleyways and into the city's maze of tall skyscrapers to avoid taking overwhelming firepower from the Bulldog tanks and Calliopes. Approach the door only after all

Figure 10.10

Approach each armory bunker only after all defenses are down.

defenses are down. The front door is colored differently than the rest of the armory. Blast it open with laser-based weaponry to reveal the armory contents and, hopefully, the presence of the weapons cache.

Maneuver your 'Mech to the three navigation points and clear all defenses surrounding each individual armory bunker. Then blow off the doors to expose the contents. When one armory bunker remains unsearched, a new lance of enemy 'Mechs arrives. It's Jeanine Castro (piloting a custom-built Daishi) and a lance of Mad Cat and Mad Cat MK. II BattleMechs here to teach you another "lesson." Retreat from their position and lure the enemy to you. Attack with long-range weaponry as they approach and order lancemates against the nearest enemy threat.

Castro and her lance are extremely tough. Be aggressive against the Mad Cats; it's unlikely that you'll need to salvage these 'Mechs. Keep your lancemates occupied with an enemy and push for a quick kill against your current target. Castro and the Mad Cat MK. II offer the greatest challenge. Gang up on her with all three lancemates until her 'Mech and her lance is destroyed.

The mission concludes in success once all defending 'Mechs are destroyed and the bunkers have been searched. Uncovering the weapons cache and capturing the enemy supplies sets the stage for the game's final mission and palace confrontation.

alternate solution

Clear out defenses around each bunker before blowing off the doors and searching through the interior contents. Knock out these defenses (which include Bulldog tanks and Calliope turrets) to face less firepower when encountering Castro's Daishi and her lance of Mad Cat and Mad Cat MK. II BattleMechs.

operation 7: "Final Victory" mission

This is what the resistance has fought so hard for. The time has come to assault the Steiner palace and its powerful 'Mech guards. Using intel gathered from the university headquarters in the previous operation, the resistance has managed to shut down the Calliope turrets surrounding the palace. Orders are to infiltrate the building, defeat its guards, level the turret power generator, and destroy Roland's dropship before it can escape.

This chapter includes the complete walkthrough for the game's concluding operation, "Final Victory." You won't find easy kills here. Elite heavy 'Mechs provide impressive palace defenses. You'll have three lancemates as well as a game's worth of salvage at your disposal. There's no holding back here. Use whatever means necessary to complete the "End Game" mission objectives. All skills gained thus far must be utilized here in order to survive this final encounter.

Operation 7, Mission 1: End Game

Mission Briefing: It is time to bring an end to this war. Enemy forces will be heavy and desperate. Your targets are the turret control facility and the dropship containing your uncle. Terminate all units to bring this war to an end.

MechLab

This final mission inside the Steiner palace is, as you might expect, also the toughest faced thus far. The elite guards are extremely skilled and are all piloting heavy, powerful 'Mechs. The terrain is mostly featureless, apart from a few hills and trees. Palace walls and internal structures, however, provide effective cover against the enemy BattleMechs. Survival requires expert lancemate use and the ability to conduct "favorable" battles against just one or two enemies at the same time.

Don't hold back—this is the final mission. Select the most powerful 'Mech salvaged thus far for yourself, which should be the devastating Daishi. Don't hesitate to stick to personal preferences. For instance, if you prefer the power of Autocannons over Gauss or PPC devices, select your 'Mech and its weaponry accordingly. You'll have a chance to repair and rearm before the mission's final battle, so keep that in mind as you choose to equip your 'Mech with ammunition- or laser-based weapons.

Battle Plan

Objectives: Destroy turret generator at NAV Beta. Stop the dropship from taking off. Take out all elite guard 'Mechs.

You begin the final mission just outside the palace grounds. A large, tall wall surrounds the interior of the palace. An entrance must be located to get inside. You're told that one lies at NAV point Alpha. Your eventual goal, Roland's dropship, lies inside the grounds. Elite 'Mech guards patrol here and many Calliope turrets are scattered around the palace, both inside and outside.

As you arrive, you get word that another infiltration team has cut turret power and the Calliope gun emplacements will be deactivated for 30 minutes. In order to remove the turrets from the scene indefinitely, locate the turret power generator at NAV point Beta. Unfortunately, the infiltration team was wrong—the enemy manages to restart the turrets and will have the Calliopes online in approximately 10 minutes. The quantity of Calliopes positioned around the palace forces a visit to the turret power generator as soon as possible (see Figure 11.1).

Listen to mission objectives and adjust your heading toward NAV Alpha. Order your lancemates to assume formation as you move toward the palace grounds entrance. Elite 'Mech guards are patrolling the area. A Nova Cat will likely appear on radar first. 'Mech opposition is extremely difficult in this mission. Stop your 'Mech and attempt to fire upon the Nova Cat at long range (with missiles or Large Lasers) to lure it (and potentially a nearby second Nova Cat) away from the palace and toward your defensive position. Order all lancemates against the approaching 'Mech. There's no need to be concerned with salvage here, so go for the quick kill by aiming at the head or heavily damaged chest areas.

Stick close to your lancemates in order to concentrate fire on later-arriving enemy 'Mechs. Separating yourself from the lance group could prove costly if you become overwhelmed by the elite 'Mech guards. There are no pushover 'Mechs here—all are heavy, durable, and come packing powerful weaponry. Avoid entering battles where you're outnumbered. Remain close to your lancemates and join them in concentrated fire against the same enemy 'Mech. Advancing further into the palace triggers an enemy Mad Cat, Thor, and powerful Daishi.

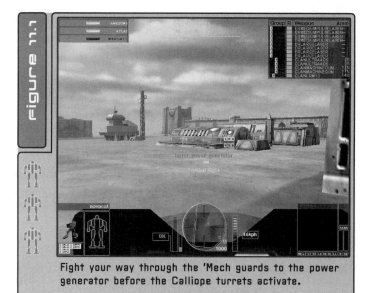

figure 11.1

Fight your way through the 'Mech guards to the power generator before the Calliope turrets activate.

Remain outside the palace as you battle the exterior guards. Move toward NAV Alpha as soon as all hostiles are crippled or eliminated. Continue ordering your lancemates to attack the nearest 'Mech as you assist. Advance to the palace and NAV Alpha. Resume your battle there until most 'Mechs are left immobile or destroyed. Cycle to NAV point Beta to pinpoint the turret power generator's location. Enter the alcove at NAV Beta and leave other structures standing (especially the 'Mech Repair Bays) as you can utilize them later in the mission.

WARNING

The Daishi is an incredible 'Mech fighting machine. Take LRMs and remain 800 meters away from it at all times. Nearly all of the Daishi's long-range firepower is limited to about this distance. Place your 'Mech in reverse and stay out of its range. Pummel the threatening 'Mech from this safe distance until it's crippled or destroyed.

Shift your crosshairs onto the turret power generator and level the structure with your laser weaponry. Don't waste many missiles or ballistics here. Monitor your radar for any remaining elite 'Mech guards. If you've been followed inside, resume combat here against the enemy 'Mechs and order lancemates to your position and into the battle. With the turret power generator destroyed, the Calliope turrets can't come online and will remain harmless for the duration of the mission.

Cycle through enemy targets until you locate the dropship. It can be found resting on a landing pad deep inside the palace grounds (see Figure 11.2). Keep your lancemates engaged with the remaining opposition 'Mech targets while you seek out the dropship. Hammer it with your beam weapons, con-

Figure 11.2

Destroying Roland's dropship completes the main objective—but doesn't end the mission. Prepare yourself for one final battle!

serving ballistic- and missile-based ammunition for use against any remaining BattleMechs. Destroy the dropship and finish off any remaining 'Mech guards to complete the mission's three objectives.

A final cutscene now plays. You're told that usable 'Mech Repair Bays can be found at NAV Delta, Epsilon, and Theta. Though it appears that the mission is complete, a new voice can suddenly be heard over the communications system—it's William! You have one more battle to finish off the war and complete the game.

When you regain control of your 'Mech, cycle to NAV Delta and use the Repair Bay to restore your 'Mech to its pristine,

NOTE

William's Daishi is custom-built and varies greatly from the default weapon and equipment layout. This Daishi has an ER PPC, 2 ER Large Pulse Lasers, 5 ER Medium Pulse Lasers, 24 heat sinks, and extremely thick reflective armor. Keeping your distance and using long-range weaponry is the best strategy to keep the bank of five Medium Pulse Lasers out of play.

pre-mission condition. William, in a powerful Daishi, waits for you just outside the palace interior.

You won't have the luxury of lancemates during this climactic encounter. William must be defeated alone. Don't charge toward his 'Mech and initiate a close-range encounter. The Daishi is extremely powerful and, as you learned earlier, best fought from a distance. Stay back and use Long-Range Missiles or lasers. Take advantage of nearby palace structures for cover. Fire an alpha strike at the Daishi's head or chest or cripple a leg to immobilize William. The mission and game end in success once all objectives have been completed and William's Daishi has been destroyed. Congratulations, MechWarrior!

Alternate Solution

The enemy Thor 'Mechs are powered down at the Repair Bays in the back of the military section of the base. Order your lancemates against active enemy 'Mech targets so you can reach the shutdown Thors quickly. Destroy or significantly weaken the Thors before they can power up.

Also, use caution when assaulting the dropship to minimize damage to your 'Mech. Stay on the plateau above the vessel so only the top portion is visible. This allows you to destroy the dropship without it firing back since all of the dropship's guns are mounted around its equator.

part 4

multiplayer
strategies

*T*his part of the guide transports you to the online battlefield of MechWarrior 4: Vengeance—intense multiplayer free-for-all and team play games. Multiplayer 'Mech combat is challenging, even if you've completed combat training, studied statistics and tactics for 'Mechs and weapons, and conquered the single-player campaign. The next two chapters outline the skills you need to survive against cunning human opponents in both solo and team competition.

Chapter 12 offers strategies for one-on-one and free-for-all games. Here you'll learn how to handle unpredictable human opponents. This chapter also includes a complete run-down of multiplayer free-for-all game types for MechWarrior 4, including Attrition, Destruction, King of the Hill, and Steal the Beacon, along with approaches for conquering each. Chapter 13 shifts the focus to team games. Strategies are presented for Capture the Flag, Team Destruction, Escort, and Team King of the Hill games.

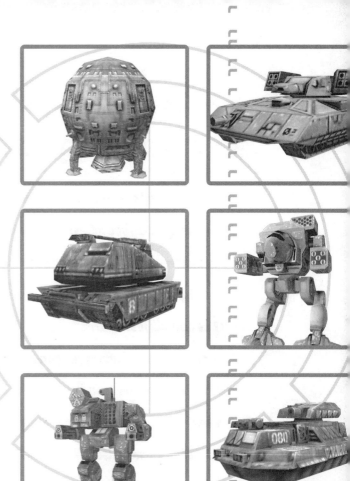

chapter 12

free-for-all strategies

You've just emerged over the hill and have spotted two heavy BattleMechs engaged in battle ahead. Quickly you adjust your weapon groupings and bind Long-Range Missiles and Large Lasers. You cycle through both enemy heavy 'Mech targets and notice via your head-up display (HUD) that one is near crumbling—its legs have been almost blown off and it has already lost an arm.

Destruction is the name of the game here. You receive points for 'Mech kills and you're about to score an easy one. Missiles are locked and Large Lasers are charged, but just as you're about to pounce, your BattleMech is rocked by PPC fire from its blind side. The sound of an enemy missile lock is the last noise you hear as your 'Mech explodes from within. Seconds away from a sure kill, you now find yourself in a fresh 'Mech but well behind the leaders on the all-important scoreboard.

Such is the world of MechWarrior 4: Vengeance's free-for-all multiplayer gaming. Featuring several game modes and intense combat, surviving a free-for-all game here requires knowledge of locational damage, weapons, combat maneuvers, and situational analysis. This chapter details strategies specific to free-for-all multiplayer modes, and the offensive tactics covered apply to both free-for-all and team battle situations.

Multiplayer Combat Basics

MechWarrior 4 multiplayer combat is much different than facing the computer-controlled 'Mechs in the single-player campaign. Although the computer AI is crafty, human opponents will be even smarter. For instance, while computer 'Mechs can be tricked and lured into ambushes, don't expect to consistently fool a human adversary.

This section covers the differences between battling a computer-controlled 'Mech and a human opponent in a multiplayer game. Incorporate these combat basics into your repertoire to both survive battles and conquer other 'Mechs in hopes of attaining the top spot on the leaderboard.

'Mech Control and Maneuvers

Effective BattleMech control is the foundation for sound multiplayer tactics. Though it's possible to get away with sheer brute force aggression against computer-controlled 'Mechs, you must employ more finesse against human opponents. Running straight at human enemies makes you an easy target. Passing by such an opponent without twisting your torso and firing off additional shots will put you at a distinct disadvantage. Expect these foes to be highly skilled in combat—therefore, you must be highly skilled yourself!

One of the most important combat concepts to grasp is the art of the "Circle of Death." This tactic, long used in the BattleTech universe, means to move in a circular pattern around your opponent while maintaining your crosshairs on the enemy—and in the case of 'Mechs, maintaining your crosshairs on the same *location* on the enemy (see Figure 12.1).

Effective implementation of the Circle of Death means moving around an enemy 'Mech,

Figure 12.1

Practice the Circle of Death by simultaneously moving, twisting, targeting, and firing—all while keeping your crosshairs on the same spot.

twisting your torso, and targeting significantly damaged areas on the enemy (or weak areas such as arms, legs, or the head). If the enemy 'Mech remains stationary, you may be able to run around the enemy faster than it can maintain a lock on you. Adjust your speed on the fly in order to keep your 'Mech just out of the enemy's line of fire. The Circle of Death permits movement around the side and rear of enemy BattleMechs, areas where they can't readily return fire.

Improving the online Performance of MechWarrior 4: Vengeance

Internet latency, or ping rate, plays an important role in online multiplayer combat. Ping rate is the time, in milliseconds, required for your computer to exchange information with the server or host. The higher the ping number, the slower the exchange. A high ping rate could have a serious effect on your online games, making enemy 'Mechs seem to jump around the screen and causing weapons to take longer than they should to discharge.

Look for the lowest ping rate when searching for a *MechWarrior 4* server. A low ping will almost always facilitate smoother online performance. As a general rule, don't join a server with a ping greater than 500 milliseconds. Connection speed, both yours and the server host's, is the largest factor in determining ping time. To improve your rate, make sure that no other Internet programs are currently active or increase your Internet connection speed. Investigate the availability of cable modems or DSL in your area. You'll find that these connections will offer significant multiplayer gaming performance improvement over dial-up Internet access.

Intelligent 'Mech control also means utilizing the environment to your advantage. Observe the terrain closely and be ready at all times to retreat behind nearby hills or use structures for cover. You're most vulnerable when exposed in an open clearing, as any player in the game can fire weapons at you. If your 'Mech is heavily damaged, expect multiple human opponents to target you.

TIP

Consider ramming! *MechWarrior 4*'s 'Mech combat includes ramming damage. The faster your 'Mech is moving at the time of collision, the more damage is inflicted. Attempt to strike the most heavily damaged areas; ramming damage is spread across body parts struck by the collision. This works particularly well for heavy 'Mechs. The heavier your 'Mech, the more damage you'll do!

Remain behind structures or near hills to give yourself an easy retreat option, both by moving forward and backward.

Realizing that retreat is an option can provide a sudden shift in battle dynamics. Consider this battle situation. Your 'Mech is damaged and under fire from an aggressive opponent. Fortunately, you're still mobile and a stationary building can be seen nearby. Retreat behind the structure, making sure to place it between you and your enemy. Twist your torso and adjust your heading to face the targeted pursuer. Keep your crosshairs at the desired target position on the reticle, such as near the bottom if the legs are heavily damaged or near the center if the enemy 'Mech has taken extensive torso damage.

When the enemy 'Mech rounds the building, discharge all weaponry at it in an alpha strike. Flush coolant if you overheat and continue moving around the building to keep out of the opponent's line of fire. It's likely you wouldn't have survived a toe-to-toe battle, but effective retreating and the alpha strike on your opponent has given you a fighting chance.

Don't ignore terrain effects on 'Mechs. For instance, snow and swamp terrain slows 55- to 75-ton BattleMechs by 25% and 75-ton or greater 'Mechs by 50%. Consider this when selecting your BattleMech. Water also has an effect on combat situations. Moving through water slows down a 'Mech, but also improves heat sink efficiency up to 200%. Take a battle to the water if your 'Mech is loaded with hot, energy-based weaponry (see Figure 12.2).

Figure 12.2

Use nearby sources of water to improve heat sink efficiency.

Smart Targeting

Targeting skills play an extremely important role no matter which multiplayer game you're playing. When you first appear in the multiplayer arena, it isn't always wise to simply target the nearest enemy 'Mech. Instead, selectively engage adversaries on the map. Cycle through your opponents and gauge their relative strengths (compared to your own 'Mech), their remaining weapons, and their distance from your 'Mech, as well as their current damage levels and where that damage lies.

In order to reach the top of the leaderboard in combat-oriented free-for-all games (Attrition and Destruction), it's important to attack enemy 'Mechs quickly. It does you no good to remain away from adversaries as others rack up kills in the heat of battle. Cycle through the targets to discover the nearest, most heavily damaged 'Mech and engage it immediately with long-range weaponry. Initiate preferred combat maneuvers (including the Circle of Death described earlier in this chapter) when you reach close range.

Look for opportunities to engage an enemy 'Mech (or multiple 'Mechs) already distracted by another battle. You'll happen upon these situations frequently, and you must capitalize on them to ensure a high placing on the current game's scoreboard. For instance, two human opponents are circling each other and dispersing dozens of weapon rounds into each other's armor plating. Both 'Mechs may be accumulating critical damage. Look for these situations. You could fire two quick Autocannon rounds into each and destroy them both. Although you did the least amount of work, smart targeting gained you the most reward: kills and points.

> **TIP**
>
> If an enemy 'Mech shows red level damage in the legs and chest area, target the legs before attacking the chest. The legs carry weaker armor than the chest. Furthermore, leg damage slows a 'Mech down—this will put you at a distinct advantage as you accelerate in for the kill.

Weapon Management

Take the time to adjust weapon groupings if the default settings don't suit your tastes. Though it's likely you would want to group short-range weapons together and long-range weapons together, it's also advantageous to create additional groupings with just beam weapons or missiles. This way you can avoid long-range beam weapon discharge (because of overheating concerns) and fire only Long-Range Missiles (see Figure 12.3).

Heat levels are directly related to your BattleMech's weapons discharge. You're a sitting duck when forced to shut down. Chronic overheating can even cause ammunition to explode. Of course, neither is desirable during frenetic multiplayer combat.

Flush coolant throughout your 'Mech (defaults to the "F" key) to keep heat levels down. Group weapons strategically, as described above, to further regulate the amount of heat generated from weapons fire.

Other than heat level concerns, there's no reason to hold back during 'Mech-to-'Mech combat. If killed, you return to the battlefield inside a fresh 'Mech with restored ammunition and weapons. You don't take leftover ammunition with you after a respawn, so make use of it while you can!

Equip your BattleMech with ammunition-based weaponry (missiles and ballistics) and fire them generously at enemy 'Mechs. Ballistics are especially powerful and can rip through armor and tear off limbs quickly. A key to multiplayer success is balancing generous weapon discharge with your 'Mech's heat levels and targeting accuracy. Firing off dozens of Autocannon rounds is meaningless if all your shots are missing their mark.

figure 12.3

Place missiles and beam weapons in separate groupings to keep heat levels down.

NOTE

Turn to Chapter 4: Weapons and Components of this guide to brush up on weapon ranges, heat levels, and relative damage potential. Understanding each of your BattleMech's weapons (as well as the weapons of your opponent) is vital. Careful study of *MechWarrior* 4's arsenal helps in both offensive and defensive situations.

Free-for-All Game Modes

Though general combat tactics will serve you well in each of *MechWarrior 4: Vengeance*'s free-for-all game modes, it's also vital to understand the rules and scoring for each game and how to apply new strategies to specific game modes.

This section covers specific strategies for *MechWarrior 4*'s free-for-all game modes, including Attrition, Destruction, King of the Hill, and Steal the Beacon.

Attrition

Objective: Points are awarded for all damage dealt. Bonuses are given out for internal damage and destroying an enemy 'Mech based on tonnage.

Table 12.1: Attrition Scoring Table

Action	Points Awarded
Point of damage inflicted on opponent	+1
Destroying enemy's internal system	+50
Destroying enemy 'Mech	+500 + Tonnage Bonus
Tonnage bonus for kills	(Target tonnage − Attacker tonnage) x 5 = Bonus (if negative, then bonus = 0)
Point of self-inflicted damage	−1
Destroying own internal component	−50
Destroying own 'Mech	−2,000

It's your 'Mech against all others in Attrition. Points are awarded based on damage inflicted, though you receive a much higher bonus if you're able to destroy an enemy 'Mech. It's wise to take shots on all enemy 'Mechs in order to score points, but it will be extremely difficult to remain near the top of the leaderboard without accumulating kills.

BattleMech tonnage greatly affects the kill bonuses in Attrition. For instance, if you're piloting a 55-ton 'Mech and destroy a 75-ton 'Mech, the tonnage bonus equals $(75-55) \times 5 = 20 \times 5 = 100$. This tonnage bonus is added to the base 500 points for each 'Mech kill. It doesn't pay to pilot smaller BattleMechs in Attrition; though you will be faster, your armor will be lighter and your weapons weaker. You're also not penalized for piloting a heavy 'Mech. Killing smaller 'Mechs provides no bonus, not even on the negative side of the ledger.

It's to your advantage to remain in the thick of the action as much as possible. Constantly fire upon enemy 'Mechs to score damage points, and target limbs and shoulders in hopes of knocking out a critical internal system. Go for those 500-point kills as often as possible, though. Monitor enemy targets frequently and prey on heavily damaged 'Mechs to steal kills from other players.

Destruction

Objective: A single point, or "frag" in first-person shooter terms, is awarded for destroying an enemy 'Mech. Two points are deducted from your score for destroying your own 'Mech.

Table 12.2: Destruction Scoring Table

Action	Points Awarded
Killing opponent	1
Suicide	-2

The rules for Destruction mode are much like traditional free-for-all first-person shooter games. You receive one point per kill and a deduction for committing an inadvertent (or even purposeful) suicide. In the case of Destruction, you lose two points for each self-kill.

Preying on weak 'Mechs is key to Destruction success (see Figure 12.4). It's difficult, not to mention time-consuming, to go toe to toe with an equivalent or greater enemy 'Mech. Instead, cycle through targets often and seek out damaged opponents.

NOTE: Suicides can occur when attempting to ram another 'Mech and you suffer too much damage in the collision. Obviously, staying near the top of the leaderboard means avoiding self-damage and self-kills. Use ramming damage tactics when you're assured of the kill, such as when inside a healthy, heavier 'Mech than your weaker opponent.

Look for enemies with red armor, indicating heavy damage, especially in the leg or chest area. Such heavy damage means that an enemy 'Mech is ripe for the kill. Adjust your heading and move in quickly.

Monitor radar blips and search for battles in progress. Approach distracted enemy 'Mechs from the side or rear—this keeps you out of the foe's line of sight and line of fire. Rear armor is also generally weaker than the front. Target the rear midsection to knock out critical systems or aim for the legs to slow down or cripple the opposing 'Mech. Ensure that you

Figure 12.4

Track down damaged enemies to score points easier and faster.

score a kill by unleashing a barrage of weapons. Work quickly to prevent another player from moving in and stealing your points.

King of the Hill

Objective: The hill is an area marked by a beacon or building (and extending in a 100-meter radius around it) in the map's center. When a player is on the hill, an icon appears in that player's head-up display (HUD). The hill is contested when more than one player stands there at the same time. When only one player is on the hill, that player has captured it until another player assumes control.

Action	Points Awarded
TABLE 12.3: KING OF THE HILL SCORING TABLE	
Contesting the hill	+1 per second
Capturing the hill	+5 per second
Killing enemy 'Mech	0

Move toward the hill as soon as possible. No points are awarded for destroying enemy 'Mechs, so it's in your best interests to avoid an early fight and begin battling for the central hill immediately. Engage in battle only when contesting the hill, which awards one point per second. Destroying contesting enemy 'Mechs will enable a full capture, which awards five points per second.

Avoid moving too far away from the hill. Should enemy 'Mechs attack you from long range, adjust your heading to place the hill between yourself and the enemy attacker. Avoid retreating, as you can't score King of the Hill points unless contesting.

Fighting should occur primarily when defending the hill. Utilize long-range weaponry (PPCs or LRMs) to fend off approaching attackers. Keep ballistic weapons handy for close-range encounters. Don't stand still; remain in motion at all times, as a moving target is more difficult to hit.

The longer you remain on the hill, the more points you score. Should your 'Mech perish, return to the hill immediately upon respawning. Target enemy 'Mechs contesting the hill as you approach and weaken them in preparation for a close-range assault.

Steal the Beacon

Objective: This mode is basically Capture the Flag without a home base. A player grabs the beacon, which starts in the center of the map, and scores one point for every second that the device is held. The beacon teleports back to the map's center if unclaimed for 30 seconds.

Table 12.4: Steal the Beacon Scoring Table

Action	Points Awarded
Holding beacon	+1 per second

Like King of the Hill, points aren't scored for kills but by completing the game mode's primary objective. Fast 'Mechs will certainly give you a noteworthy advantage. You can grab the beacon quickly, then move away from enemy 'Mechs and use the environment (hills and structures) as cover. Faster generally means weaker, though. It's possible that a lighter, quicker 'Mech won't be able to survive for long once harassed by its larger cousins.

You'll become the main target after acquiring the beacon. Though some other fighting may occur, most enemy 'Mechs will be coming after you (see Figure 12.5). Use the radar to identify

NOTE

If you shut down your 'Mech with the beacon in hand, it is immediately dropped and can be claimed by another player. Watch heat levels carefully so you aren't forced to do this. Shut down only if you're positioned far from enemy 'Mechs.

their location and incoming trajectories. Torso-twist as much as you can and fire long-range weaponry at the approaching rivals. Adjust your heading from side to side to present a more difficult target. Place any sort of environmental feature between you and pursuing 'Mechs to carry the beacon as long as possible. Check your six and run for dear life!

Figure 12.5

You've got the beacon—expect to be immediately targeted and attacked!

team play strategies

In MechWarrior 4: Vengeance's free-for-all games, you aren't dependent on anyone. Each 'Mech on the map is an enemy. In team games, however, you're given 'Mechs who assist you in battle. With this assistance comes responsibility, though. Each team member is dependent on the other to maintain focus on game objectives and to accomplish specific tasks along the path to victory.

This chapter covers tactics specific to MechWarrior 4: Vengeance's team play game modes, including Team Attrition, Capture the Flag, Team Destruction, Escort, and Team King of the Hill. Techniques specific to team games are also covered. Over the following pages, you'll learn the importance of communication and concentrated fire, where teammates attempt to ensure a consistent win by double- or triple-teaming enemy 'Mechs.

Team Play Basics

While nearly all free-for-all combat techniques apply to team play situations, there are specific tactics to remember when engaged in team 'Mech warfare. Without them, a team becomes disorganized and won't be able to consistently win victories. An organized group applying important team play techniques is nearly invulnerable against a less organized opponent. This section illustrates key team play concepts, including communication and concentrated fire. Both are vital to consistent team play success.

Effective Communication

Unlike free-for-all game modes, where it's every 'Mech for itself, team games rely on coordination and, naturally, teamwork. In order to achieve these, a team must rely heavily on communication. The primary way to coordinate an attack, set up a solid defense, or accomplish a secret maneuver is to open the lines of communication between teammates.

Be prepared to chat frequently to relay your 'Mech status to teammates, report the position of an enemy offensive, or request additional defensive support. Communication encompasses every aspect of team games. A team without communication simply can't compete with an organized opponent (see Figure 13.1).

Filter out useless chat, however, and stick firmly to the game situation at hand. Don't talk about real-world current events when you should be discussing the heavy 'Mech bearing down on your defensive position.

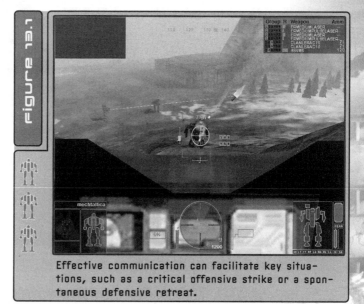

Figure 13.1

Effective communication can facilitate key situations, such as a critical offensive strike or a spontaneous defensive retreat.

Concentrated Fire

One of the most important aspects of team play is concentrated fire. This is where you attempt to orchestrate favorable matchups for your team. You should always seek out situations where you can outnumber the enemy team at the point of attack. For instance, send two or three or however many 'Mechs you can spare against individual enemies.

'Mech-to-'Mech battles take time and can often lead to extended stalemates, especially if the 'Mechs are of like size and the pilots of similar skill. Two-on-one situations, however, are extremely difficult to overcome—even if it involves two light or medium 'Mechs against a single heavy unit. While one BattleMech occupies the enemy's forward fire, the other can attack the weaker rear armor or concentrate solely on breaking off an arm or crushing a leg.

Just as you would in a free-for-all situation, prey on weaker 'Mechs. Cycle through the targets and engage not the nearest enemy 'Mech, but the nearest and weakest enemy 'Mech. Take battles to the opposing team by doubling up attackers. Monitor friendly units and their current target. Order stronger teammates against weaker targets to maintain an advantage.

TIP

In Capture the Flag and Escort games, push forward to the team's defending position and keep combat focused there. If the opposing team is forced to defend constantly, it becomes very difficult to mount an offense and win the game.

Team Play Game Modes

Consistently winning team games requires an understanding of specific game rules and scoring. It's also vital to employ specific *MechWarrior 4* tactics to each specific team game.

This section covers specific strategies for team play game modes, including Team Attrition, Capture the Flag, Team Destruction, Escort, and Team King of the Hill.

NOTE

Refer to Chapter 12: Free-for-All Strategies to learn specific 'Mech-to-'Mech battle techniques. This style of combat is an integral part of team games, too. Use the tactics described in both Chapter 12 and this one to improve your game and your team's chances of winning.

Team Attrition

Objective: Team points are awarded for all damage inflicted on the enemy team's 'Mechs. Larger bonuses are given for destroying internal systems and destroying an enemy 'Mech completely. Points are deducted for self-damage, suicides, and friendly-fire kills.

Table 13.1: Team Attrition Scoring Table

Action	Points Awarded
Point of damage inflicted on opponent	+1
Destroying enemy's internal system	+50
Destroying enemy 'Mech	+500 + Tonnage Bonus
Tonnage bonus for kills	(Target tonnage – Attacker tonnage) x 5 = Bonus (if negative, then bonus = 0)
Point of self-inflicted damage	–1
Destroying own internal component	–50
Destroying own 'Mech	–2,000
Killing teammate	–500

Because you receive team points by simply inflicting damage on enemy 'Mechs, get moving into the battle action quickly (see Figure 13.2). Utilize long-range weaponry, specifically PPCs, Gauss devices, Large Lasers, or LRMs, to attack enemy 'Mechs from long range (such as when approaching the map's central area from the outlying respawn points). Though all damage scores points, kills accumulate much faster. Seek out damaged enemy 'Mechs and concentrate fire on them instead of simply the nearest enemy 'Mech or a healthy enemy 'Mech.

Move into the battle quickly but wisely. Concentrate fire on damaged enemy 'Mechs first—specifically heavier damaged 'Mechs.

A tonnage bonus is added to each enemy kill based on your 'Mech's tonnage and the enemy 'Mech's tonnage. If you're piloting a smaller 'Mech, you'll receive a bonus to the base 500 points. Place two team members in smaller but well-armed 'Mechs (as best as the MechLab will allow) and order them to concentrate fire on the same enemy heavy BattleMech each round. Though the heavy 'Mech is more powerful, it's difficult to combat two 'Mechs at once—especially when they're fast. Go for the heavy BattleMech's legs quickly to slow it down even further.

Capture the Flag

Objective: Every team in the game possesses a single flag located in the center of its base. Enemy flags must be returned to the player's team base (brought inside the 100-meter circular flag area) to receive points. If the flag carrier shuts down or is destroyed, the flag is ejected. If the flag is not picked up again within 30 seconds, it teleports back to the owning team's base.

WARNING

Suicides cost your team an enormous amount of points. Avoid ramming damage unless you're assured victory. Watch your heat carefully and shut down or use coolant as necessary. Overheating your 'Mech can cause internal explosions and possible destruction.

Table 13.2: Capture the Flag Scoring Table

Action	Points Awarded
Flag capture	1,000
Killing opponent	25
Killing teammate	-50

One of the most important aspects of Capture the Flag is designating team duties. A team leader should request that a few members remain near the home base to defend the flag position. A couple of players (or more depending on the game size) should pilot faster, lighter 'Mechs and attempt to snag the enemy flag. Heavier 'Mechs should defend their lighter counterparts and attempt to punch a hole through the enemy base defenses. Capture the Flag is one of the all-time great team-oriented games, and success requires communication, concentration, and a keen sense of offense and defense.

TIP

Employ concentrated fire (outnumbering single enemy targets) and flanking maneuvers to clear base defenders. This will allow speedy 'Mechs the chance to get inside and snatch the flag.

Defenders should pilot heavy 'Mechs. Speed isn't a necessity, as defenders should stay close to their home base. Arm defenders with mostly long-range beam and missile-based weaponry. Outfit some close-range devices in case attackers break through and threaten your flag. Target incoming enemy 'Mechs and weaken them with long-range blasts to make grabbing your flag a difficult chore.

Offensive players hoping to grab enemy flags will find success manning quick, light 'Mechs with an emphasis on maneuverability. This means that medium and heavy 'Mechs are needed to accompany and defend the flag grabbers. They'll be needed to distract or destroy enemy defenses to give their allies a chance at emerging from the fray successfully.

Team Destruction

Objective: One point is awarded for killing enemy team 'Mechs. Friendly-fire kills and suicide deaths are punished through point deductions.

Table 13.3: Team Destruction Scoring Table

Action	Points Awarded
Killing opponent	1
Killing teammate	-1
Suicide	-2

Unlike Team Attrition, points are awarded only for kills. Thus, you must be somewhat more cautious during team and individual attacks. Furthermore, there are no tonnage bonuses, so don't hesitate to prey on lighter enemy 'Mechs. In fact, it's a good strategy to coordinate attacks with teammates against weaker opponents. Two heavier 'Mechs can eliminate a smaller rival in no time (see Figure 13.3). The main challenge is keeping up with the faster 'Mech. Use the Circle of Death technique

Figure 13.3

Bully weaker 'Mechs and gang up on them. There's no tonnage bonus—simply one point per enemy kill!

CHAPTER 13: TEAM PLAY STRATEGIES

(described in Chapter 12: Free-for-All Strategies) and twist your torso to maintain your crosshairs on the target. Consider having one teammate ram the smaller 'Mech while the other teammate fires weapons—but be careful to avoid friendly fire!

Seek out two-on-one or three-on-one situations as often as possible. Going toe to toe with each enemy 'Mech takes time and serves no purpose if you're just exchanging kill points with the enemy. Look for teammates engaged in battle and assist them by attacking the opponent from the rear or side. Blow off a limb or cripple a leg. Communicate frequently and instruct teammates to either prepare for your arrival (to be wary of friendly fire) or to assist against a strong enemy 'Mech.

Escort

Objective: One player is designated as the game's VIP. Other players must escort that VIP into the score zone to receive points. Escorts will attempt to destroy the other team's VIP before it reaches the score zone.

Table 13.4: Escort Scoring Tables

VIP Action	Points Awarded
1st score zone	1,000
2nd score zone	2,000
3rd score zone	4,000
4th score zone	8,000 (score continues to double after each additional score zone reached—i.e., fifth score zone reached equals 16,000 points and so on)

Escort Action	Points Awarded
Killing enemy 'Mech	100
Killing teammate	-100
Killing enemy VIP	500
Killing own VIP	-1,000
Suicide	-100

Delegating duties plays a huge role in Escort, a unique *MechWarrior 4: Vengeance* game mode where teammates must escort a player designated as the VIP back and forth between score zones. A good strategy is to assign specific players to closely defend the VIP from attack while others remain farther scouting and engaging enemy 'Mechs or the enemy VIP. Patrol safety zones and clear out defenses to make way for the VIP escort.

Keep heavy 'Mechs around your VIP, both to absorb damage and to aggressively repel attacks. Scouts should occupy medium 'Mechs, adding maneuverability at the cost of some armor and firepower. Press enemy VIP and safety zone positions with a heavy 'Mech force and concentrate fire on damaged enemies to destroy them quickly. Place 'Mechs between the VIP and enemy BattleMechs' line of fire to serve as a shield or as the last line of protection should the friendly VIP near the score zone.

WARNING

Avoid friendly fire at all costs, especially in close-range VIP defense. Killing your own VIP deducts 1,000 points from the team's total; this could mean the difference between victory and failure in a tightly contested game. More importantly, the VIP's death takes away the all-important multiplier.

Team King of the Hill

Objective: A beacon or building in the center of the map is designated as the hill. Teams are awarded points by contesting or capturing the hill (walking within a 100-meter radius around the beacon or building). If two players on the same team are the only two 'Mechs on the hill, you receive one point per second per player. Only if you have five or more players on the hill does the team begin to receive the full capture award of five points per second.

Table 13.5: King of the Hill Scoring Table

Action	Points Awarded
Contesting the hill	+1 per second
Capturing the hill	+5 per second
Killing enemy 'Mech	No points awarded

Though killing an enemy team member's 'Mech doesn't grant you any points, it's a good way to keep the enemy team from contesting the hill. Designate one player as the hill "contester" while other team members target aggressive incoming enemy 'Mechs attempting to capture the hill (see Figure 13.4). Follow Destruction strategies, such as concentrating the firepower of multiple team members on the same enemy 'Mech, in order to keep the challenger safe from attack.

Crowding the hill can provide a full capture, but it can also cause confusion and friendly fire. Keeping one contester on the hill should work well if other players are engaged with enemy BattleMechs. Make sure that a few teammates remain near the hill in case the contester is destroyed. You don't want to waste any time away from the hill. As soon as a contester is destroyed, order another teammate to begin contesting and scoring points immediately.

Figure 13.4

The hill contester sticks close to the building and scores points while other team members defend the position from enemy aggression.